— THE —

STRATEGIC DIVIDEND INVESTOR

DANIEL PERIS

New York   Chicago   San Francisco   Lisbon   London   Madrid   Mexico City
Milan   New Delhi   San Juan   Seoul   Singapore   Sydney   Toronto

3 4 5 6 7 8 9 10 11 12 13 14 15   QFR/QFR   1 9 8 7 6 5 4 3 2

ISBN   978-0-07-176960-0
MHID   0-07-176960-9

This publication is designed to provide accurate and authoritative information in regard to the subject matter covered. It is sold with the understanding that neither the author nor the publisher is engaged in rendering legal, accounting, securities trading, or other professional services. If legal advice or other expert assistance is required, the services of a competent professional person should be sought.
> —*From a Declaration of Principles Jointly Adopted by a Committee of the American Bar Association and a Committee of Publishers and Associations*

Library of Congress Cataloging-in-Publication Data

Peris, Daniel.
    The strategic dividend investor / by Daniel Peris.
       p.   cm.
    Includes bibliographical references.
    ISBN 978-0-07-176960-0 (alk. paper)
    1. Dividends.   2. Investment analysis.

    HG4028.D5 P47   2011
    332.63'22—dc22   2010052539

The views and opinions expressed in this publication are those of the author and do not necessarily reflect the views or opinions of Federated Investors, Inc., or its affiliates.

For L.A.P./N.Y.P.

A cow for her milk,
A hen for her eggs,
And a stock, by heck,
For her dividends.

An orchard for fruit
Bees for their honey,
And stocks, besides,
For their dividends.

—John Burr Williams,
  The Theory of Investment Value

Contents

Preface

If you like to trade stocks, read no further. If you find the financial media—particularly the televised circus shows—to be helpful to investors, you can put this book down right now. If, however, you've come to suspect that following the advice of Wall Street to buy and sell individual stocks frequently as a core investment strategy isn't quite right, read on. If you manage your own business or own rental or commercial real estate, this analysis should speak to you. If you took a finance class in college and are puzzled why the methods taught there seem to be ignored in the stock market, read on. This book grew out of nearly daily conversations over the past several years with investors ranging from individuals of modest means to high-end consultants for large pension funds, endowments, and advisor platforms. It is designed to counter a fallacy about investing that has grown insidiously over the past few decades, so much so that the fallacy has become the "conventional wisdom." My goal is to clear the air and to help investors understand what I consider to be, and has historically been, the proper purpose and usage of stocks. I offer neither a trading strategy nor a get-rich-quick scheme. If anything, investing in dividends is a get-rich-slowly plan. Slow and steady wins the long race. For those of you who have already built up your retirement nest egg, you need a stay-rich strategy, and dividend investing is precisely that.

The focus on dividends is not new; in fact, it is old and central to how the stock market has functioned over the past two centuries. Indeed, the bookshelves of your local library hold many books about dividend investing and even more on general investing that accord a lot of attention to dividends. Some of them are quite good. So why do we need another one? Well, to judge by the events of the last decade, investors haven't been paying attention. "Playing the stock market" remains a national pastime. Indeed, the last 10 years—characterized by two stock market bubbles followed by two crashes and a series of other jarring speculations (e.g., housing, energy)—constitutes its own advertisement for the alternative of slow and steady dividend investing. So ask yourself: Are you happy with your returns from your stock market investments? Are you content with the daily, often wild swings in the value of businesses that you know to be generally stable? Are you delighted by all the complex accounting at the end of the year as you prepare your taxes? If you are reading this, the answer is probably no. And when all is said and done, the stock market is at the same level it was a decade ago. In contrast, a dividend-focused equity portfolio, where the returns were skewed to cash payments, would have easily outperformed the market, as we'll see in the section looking at historical returns.

But there is a more basic reason for reminding investors yet again why they should focus on dividends. It is the same reason that your mother repeatedly warned you against running while carrying sharp objects, why your physician frequently pesters you to lay off the fatty foods, and why organized religion offers weekly reminders of what is right and what is wrong. We humans are simply not wired to act consistently in our best long-term interests. Indeed, it is one of the defining characteristics of our species: to have the ability to reason but to choose consciously not to do so. This book is part of that eternal tug of war. Of course, determining the right thing to do can itself be very difficult, but even when we know what it is (e.g., dental floss, broccoli, exercise, moderation), the temptations (e.g., TV, pizza, self-indulgence) can be irresistible. And the rewards for doing the right thing can take longer to manifest themselves than we are willing to wait. We are unusually impatient and frequently irrational creatures, and the stock market is about as direct a reflection of that condition as can be imagined.

So to get through to multitasking, media-choked, I-want-it-now investors, this work is deliberately short and focused on delivering a simple message: that dividends dominate the components of total return; invest in dividends. It's not that complicated. The brevity is also designed to match the alarmingly brief attention span of the retail investor and financial advisor who cannot pull themselves away from their computers or TVs long enough to realize that the obsession with the here and now is at the heart of the problem in our approach to the stock market. Living your life or managing your finances while running on a human-sized hamster wheel is neither fun nor likely to be particularly effective. But even in our frantic modern lives, there is some downtime—on an airplane, in the doctor's office—and this treatment is designed to be concise enough so that you can get through it without having to make a *War and Peace*–like commitment of time.

With the same goal of making sure the message gets through, I'm keeping the endnotes to a minimum and the tone conversational rather than academic. The academics generally already know this material; it's the rest of us who need the lesson. For those of you who want to go deeper, there is a suggested reading section at the end. As much as I would like to, I cannot, however, entirely dispense with charts and reviews of quantitative studies, so some numeracy is assumed. If you stumble over those sections, each and every one can be summarized by repeating the basic mantra of this book: dividends dominate the components of total return; invest in dividends. (If you're noting that you just read that in the last paragraph, prepare yourself. In some form or another, it's going to be on every page.)

To help drive home the point, I am very conscious about not overusing the term *stock*. The popular understanding of the word itself has become part of the problem, so you will see instead a preference for terms such as *investment, security, ownership stake*, and so on. Similarly, dividends are central to my thesis, but their role is not well understood by many investors. Therefore, I frequently make my point by referring to them as distributable profits, cash distributions, and so forth. The repetition and the terminology are not accidental. Part of the challenge that retail (as opposed to institutional) investors face is working through the current meaning of many terms that they encounter. Professionals may find this approach too simplistic for their tastes, but they should at least recognize the misunderstanding that I am trying to address. As currently constituted, the financial services industry is part of the problem; hopefully, it will become part of the solution.

This treatment is distinctive in one other regard. By training and inclination, I am a historian who just happens to work by day as a mutual fund manager. My background very much frames how I approach investing in general and how dividend investing is presented here. If I draw on past stock market performance and the past record of human behavior in regard to stocks quite a bit, it's because we have seen this movie before, during the railroad speculations of the nineteenth century, during the Roaring Twenties, during the tech boom a decade ago. The historical record about those speculative periods and about the alternative of focusing on dividends is abundantly clear. History doesn't necessarily repeat itself, but there are certain patterns that can be discerned and offer us the opportunity to benefit from past experience. That same historical record shows, alas, that we rarely learn much from the mistakes of our forebears, but at least we can make the effort.

The first two chapters of the text focus on answering the "Why dividends?" question. It is at once the most historical and theoretical (about the mathematics of investment). You should read these chapters closely. I feel that they are the most important part of the book, but if neither history nor math is what you're looking for, just make sure you get this much: for most investors most of the time, dividends are the point of a public equity investment, and therefore, dividends have dominated stock market returns historically and are likely to continue dominating future equity returns. The third chapter discusses how we got to our current state of affairs, which I call "Trader Nation." Here I burn a few bridges, name names, and suggest why our 25-year drift away from dividends is likely to reverse course over the next decade. The last two chapters of the book offer a glimpse into the *how* of dividend investing. You may be tempted to jump right to these chapters to find the answer to your immediate investment question. The answer is, in fact, in the earlier chapters on *why*. Again, I urge you not to skip them. Once you understand that dividends dominate the components of total return (these terms will be fully explained in the text), the *how* chapters become a quite straightforward overview. They are not meant to be exhaustive, but to provide you with a set of analytical tools that you can use to either continue your reading or engage your financial advisor. They also include several stock stories that you can latch on to, and walk you through the financial statements of a typical dividend-focused stock. I conclude by recapping what investors need to do (it's mostly a mental exercise) to use the stock market properly and benefit from it, rather than being confused and repelled by it.

Acknowledgments

Works of this sort are almost always collaborative, and this is no exception. I want to thank first and foremost my colleagues at Federated Investors in Pittsburgh, in particular the head of our dividend investing franchise, Walter Bean, for his unstinting support over the years that we have worked together. Thanks also to Mike Granito, Debbie Bickerstaff, Patrick Lynch, Ian Miller, and Dana Meissner, and to our former colleague, Ben Klaber, for his help in analyzing market returns. More generally, Federated has offered a challenging but congenial work environment for nearly a decade, and I am especially grateful to Steve Auth and John Fisher for their willingness to harbor a fugitive historian in their midst. Beyond Federated, I am indebted to Bob Mecoy for his good counsel, and to the excellent editors at McGraw-Hill. Josh Peters of Morningstar and I have had frequent and intense discussions about dividend investing. Ian Kennedy (formerly of Cambridge Associates) and Rich Bernstein (formerly of Merrill Lynch) read and commented intelligently on earlier versions of the manuscript. These individuals, however, are not responsible for any factual or interpretive errors herein; those are all my own.

1

Why Invest for Dividends?

What Is a Dividend?

Let's start by turning off CNBC, putting down the *Wall Street Journal,* and considering what an investment really is. You are turning over money to someone or something in expectation of getting a return greater than the cost you may have incurred to raise the funds or greater than what alternate investments in a similar endeavor (e.g., stocks, bonds, real estate, private equity, or a hot dog stand) might produce. If it is structured as debt, you are lending money in return for a stated percentage from the coupon and your principal back at a later time. In the open market, the price of the principal may fluctuate somewhat, but the return that you receive is basically the coupon and then your money back. Defaults on principal are rare, and the risk of default is, in theory, priced into the principal.

Stocks are not much different. You are providing capital to management in return for a small ownership stake in the company—hence the name "equity." It is a share of the company's assets that remain after the company has satisfied its obligations, such as debt and accounts payable. Unless purchased at an initial public offering or at some other capital raising, you are generally buying your stake from a third party rather than from the company itself. Unlike debt, equity has no maturity date. The stake in the company will belong to you in perpetuity unless you sell it to someone else or the company itself is purchased or goes out of business.

A company invests the capital that it gets directly from investors however it sees fit, but with an expectation that it will generate a return greater than it spent to raise that capital. Small, early-stage companies may not have any near-term positive return. They generally should rely on the cozier and more risk-oriented world of private equity. Larger and more established companies—those whose equities are publicly traded on and dominate the stock market—will usually have a positive return from their businesses. That is, they earn profits. Depending on the industry and the company's stage of development, some of those profits will be reinvested back into the business. But the excess profits belong to the owners of the company—the shareholders—and are (or should be) distributed to them in the form of dividends. That's why people should invest in stocks: to access streams of distributable profits in the companies that they own. Why else would you want to own a stake in a large corporation if not to share in the profits and to get them in cash?

Investors have become accustomed to hearing a different answer to that question: you buy stocks because you believe that they will "go up" and you can sell them for a gain. But think about it. Stocks go up presumably because the business is worth more. A business is *necessarily* worth more if it has large and rising distributions of cash to company owners. Unless you subscribe to a vast greater-fool theory—where someone is always willing to buy something from you for more than you paid for it regardless of its "worth"—the final purchaser of a stock has to be buying the security with the expectation of holding it in perpetuity based on its intrinsic value. If you are holding a stock with no expectation of selling it, the only value it can possibly generate for you is through the cash that you receive from it: the dividends. In the daisy chain of buyers and sellers, it all comes down to cash. If the last buyer can't justify the purchase based on the cash received from holding on to the business permanently, he or she would not (should not) buy it, and the daisy chain unravels back to the first buyer.

In that regard, investing in stocks is not much different from purchasing rental property. You buy it and perhaps fix it up. That's the capital that you've invested. You lease out the apartments or the commercial space. What's left after you've paid the expenses is the return on your investment. Whether through improvements, a bit of inflation, or your savvy in choosing a property in an up-and-coming neighborhood, your rents go up modestly year after year, as does the value of the property should you choose to sell it to someone who is making the same calculation. If you don't choose to sell it, you continue to benefit from the rising stream of rents.

The basic math applies to any persons running their own business. They've put time, energy, and actual money into it. For a period they have probably endured losses and then reinvested all the early profits back into the business. (At this stage, it can be quite hard to determine what the business is really worth.) But as the business matures, they begin to take out cash distributions, and the value of the enterprise continues to grow in line with those distributions. I've often commented to our clients that if we could easily tap into the rising distributable profit streams of local private businesses—say the dry cleaner on the corner, the bakery down the street, the dentist's office by the school, for instance—we would consider it. But the reality is that to access dividend streams and to still permit investors to enter and exit in a timely fashion, we have to rely on companies where the equity is priced and available on a daily basis—the stock market. But you should not confuse the means with the end: you don't want to invest in the stock market; you want to invest in companies through the stock market. Over the past two decades, our society has made a fetish of stocks rather than seeing them for what they are: a flawed but ultimately practical means of accessing distributable profit streams from corporations in return for providing capital to those same corporations. For many investors, however, the market has become an end unto itself: a platform to try to "buy low, sell high, repeat frequently," not unlike a casino.

While the popular understanding of the stock market has evolved in recent decades, the math underlying the stock market has not. The math bears out the instrumental role of stocks and the ultimate point of investing in them: getting a regular, and where possible growing, cash payment over time. On any given day, the number of buyers and sellers and a whole host of factors external to a company itself will set the price of a stock. Determining an actual present value for those securities (i.e., what one might consider a fair price), however, involves calculating the dividend yield (the annual dividend divided by the current price), asserting the growth rate for the dividend, and coming up with an appropriate discount rate for the future income stream to take into account risks to the business and the time value of money. The latter is very important and captures the fact that $1 paid to you today is worth more than a promise to pay $1 one year from now. That is because there is still some risk that you won't get paid in a year, and the very real risk that the $1 paid then will buy less than a current dollar of goods and services.

The dividend discount model (DDM) and discounted cash flow (DCF) programs on your financial calculator and in the first chapter of the dust-covered finance textbook on your bookshelf provide a means of figuring out the present value of those future payments. The basic math is worth reviewing briefly. To determine the present value for a flat dividend stream, say $1 per year, you apply a discount rate to the future payments. Using a discount rate of 7.0% means that the annual stream of $1 payments is worth about $14 right now. In other words, all other things being equal (and they never are), a stock trading with a 7.0% dividend yield ($1 dividend/$14 price) has an assumption built into it that the payment will be made for the foreseeable future but will not grow. Anything you pay more than 14 times the coupon for an income stream (i.e., any stock having less than a 7.0% yield) is the premium for growth in the future payments. For instance, if the $1 dividend grows steadily at 4.0% a year, the present value jumps to $33. Note how much of the stock's present value—the price you might choose to pay for it—is dependent upon the growth in the income stream. The present value is equally dependent on the discount rate. For the sake of simplicity, I use the 7.0% discount rate throughout this work, but a higher discount rate, reflecting a greater risk that those future payments may not materialize or be worth less, reduces the present value. A lower one, conversely, increases it. Low discount rates can end up justifying investments where most if not all of the present value comes from those outlying years; in contrast, higher discount rates all but demand a significant *current* return—a higher dividend yield—because they quickly reduce the value of those outyear payments to very little. Note that we are currently in a period when very low discount rates are commonly applied to investments. Risk, it seems, just isn't as risky as it used to be.

Let's take an important real-world example—the Standard and Poor's (S&P) 500 Index of the leading stocks in the United States. If purchased through an index fund, the S&P 500 Index has offered investors a 2.0% or less dividend yield for the past decade. That is, for each $1 in cash received from their investment annually, investors are paying a remarkable $50. Wow! From a present value perspective using the same 7.0% discount rate, that means that less than 30% of the market's current price is captured by the dividend stream. The remaining 70% of what is being paid is based on an expectation that the market's dividend will grow by 5.0% *forever*. (Raise the discount rate to the 9.0% or so level often applied to the U.S. stock market, and the present value drops to just 22% of the market's current price. To get the very simple present value formula to support the S&P 500 Index at 1200—the level at time of printing—the dividends would have to grow at 7.0% for eternity—an unlikely prospect.) In short, at a 2.0% yield, the U.S. market isn't offering investors very much value up front, and you are counting on tremendous growth in those cash payments to justify your purchase price. In contrast, an equity portfolio with a 5.0% dividend yield covers 70% of its purchase amount through its current income stream alone. Add growth of just 2.0% in the income stream, and the portfolio's cost is fully captured by the dividends that it generates. Any increase in the income stream above 2.0% annually and the value of the investment will necessarily rise. In short, the more you get up front, the less you have to rely on the promise of growth in the future. A bird in the hand is worth two in the bush.

That's all fine you say, but the market really isn't valued on the basis of its dividends, is it? And you'd be correct, at least for the past couple of decades. Instead, most investors and commentators focus on price-to-earnings ratios (P/Es). P/Es are mathematical cousins of a discounted cash flow analysis, but there the similarity ends. The P/E takes into account not cash received by company owners but nominal profits earned by the company. In theory, a shareholder has a claim on company earnings, but as a practical matter, those profits get to you only through dividends (or if you sell the stock to someone else hoping to access those profits). Now let's look at the market from a P/E perspective. Wall Street expects the S&P 500 Index companies to have earned around $80 (per each measure of the index) in 2010. That compares to a price for the S&P 500 Index of around $1,200 as of late 2010. Therefore, the market is trading at about 15 times ($1,200/$80) expected current profits, for an earnings "yield" of 6.6% ($80/$1,200). If that were the actual cash received by investors, it would be rather attractive. But that is not the case. Viewing the market this way makes it look a lot cheaper than it in fact is. Indeed, less than 30% of those earnings are paid out in the form of dividends, which is why the market has its miserly 2.0% yield. The remaining profits are kept by management for reinvestment, share repurchases, acquisitions, and so forth. Valuing the market on the basis of P/Es and coming to the conclusion that it offers a good return makes a virtue of necessity when cash returns are so low. Critics can and will answer that the market can "support" higher valuation multiples, and therefore lower dividend yields, because interest rates are low (keeps the discount rate low) and our long-term growth prospects are good (an open society, entrepreneurial spirit, emerging market exposure, etc.)—but investors should know that when they buy a stock at a certain yield or P/E what that exactly means.

So why dividends? Two reasons. As an investor, you are taking a stake in a company, and dividends are the acid test of a business's basic profitability. If a mature enterprise claims to be a robust business but doesn't pay a significant dividend, you have to ask why. Early-stage ventures can be excluded from this expectation, but most publicly traded companies that have been around for decades should not be. The second reason is that the point of financial investment is to get a cash return. You the investor provided cash to take a stake in the first place. The dividend—not hoping to buy low, sell high, and repeat frequently in an almost unknowable environment—is the most direct, obvious, and natural form of return from equities.

Investment Versus Speculation

The point of investing in stocks may be to access cash streams, but the reality is that throughout the history of the modern equity markets (roughly the last 200 years) speculation in stocks without regard to cash payment streams (along with outright fraud, bubbles, and panics) has made up a substantial portion and at times the majority of market activity.[1] Along with many other get-rich-quick schemes, viewing the stock market as a casino where one can come away a winner overnight has been and remains an all-too-common part of modern life for many Americans. It is typical of our contemporary cultural makeup. It's the same logic that leads otherwise rational, intelligent people to purchase lottery tickets. For a dollar, you can purchase a pleasant few hours of reverie about how you'd live the life of luxury. There's nothing wrong with that, but it's not a practical means of becoming wealthy.

I'm not saying much that is new here. Almost every worthwhile analysis of the stock market begins by distinguishing between speculation and investment. John Burr Williams opened his forgotten classic, *The Theory of Investment Value*, with the succinct observation that "Separate and distinct things not to be confused, as every thoughtful investor knows, are real worth and market price."[2] For Williams, "successful speculation consists in [foreseeing changes in opinion]. It requires no knowledge of intrinsic value as such, but only of what people are going to believe intrinsic value to be. . . . How to foretell changes in opinion is the heart of the problem of speculation, just as how to foretell changes in dividends is the heart of the problem of investment."[3] In a similar vein, John Maynard Keynes wrote that speculators are "largely concerned, not with making superior long-term forecasts of the probable yield of an investment over its whole life, but with foreseeing changes in the conventional basis of valuation a short time ahead of the general public. They are concerned, not with what an investment is really worth to a man who buys it for 'keeps,' but with what the market will value it at, under the influence of mass psychology, three months or a year hence."[4]

Famed value investor Benjamin Graham devotes the entire first chapter of *The Intelligent Investor* to differentiating between investing and speculating. For him, "an investment operation is one which, upon thorough analysis promises safety of principal and an adequate return. Operations not meeting these requirements are speculative."[5] That is, Graham sets the bar high: investment is serious business; everything else is speculation. In this regard, he echoes the famous *Harvard College v. Armory* Massachusetts court decision of 1830 that defined (and still generally defines) the obligations of a fiduciary—a person responsible for managing money on someone else's behalf. That ruling directed trustees "to observe how men of prudence, discretion and intelligence manage their own affairs, not in regard to speculation, but in regard to the permanent disposition of their funds, considering the probable income, as well as the probable safety of the capital to be invested." Note the time frame and the opposition of speculation to income generation. This so-called Prudent Man Rule technically applies only to those individuals legally considered fiduciaries, but all advisors and investors should keep its tenets in mind.

In short, investing is like life. Face it soberly, and you have a better chance of doing well. Too many investors, as Benjamin Graham observed decades ago, who are quite serious in acquiring their wealth, become bizarrely indifferent as to the disposition of their hard-earned dollars: "It is amazing to see how many capable businessmen try to operate in Wall Street with complete disregard of all the sound principles through which they have gained success in their own undertakings."[6] Instead, they treat it as a separate sphere of endeavor where the analytical approach is not relevant. After years of hard work, they easily and without hesitation consign their wealth to a great casino, close their eyes, and hope for the best. For some risk takers—the skydivers of this world—that may be fine, but for the rest of us, gambling with our retirement savings is not very wise. Indeed, even the skydiver should consider a nonskydiving approach to his or her own retirement assets. Perhaps only the super rich, with vast current and future resources, can afford to treat their investments like so many poker chips ready for the green felt. This book is not for them.

As a practical matter, speculation tends to be near-term in nature with an expected gain in days, weeks, or months, while the returns from an investment tend to be framed in years. How patient are you? How often do you review your stock portfolio? Dividends don't change very often, usually just once a year. Stock prices rise and fall every day. When the market is moving strongly against your portfolio, or the market is roaring but you are not participating, it can be very difficult not to succumb to speculative thoughts. The temptation "to do something" about a portfolio that is "not working" can be great, even if that same portfolio is quietly and consistently generating rising cash payments to you. Slow down and smell the roses (count the dividend checks coming in), and stop trying to beat the casino. Do you change your job every few months, regularly shift how you raise your children, flit in and out of hobbies, or rotate religious affiliations? Most people would agree that doing so is a bad idea. Yet when it comes to the stock market, people are quite happy to show no constancy whatsoever, to make quick decisions, and then reverse them just as rashly. Those investors pay a price for all their back-and-forth motion. Most individual investors in the U.S. stock market do far worse than the market's average 9.0%–10% annual return because of their tendency to move in and out of investments at just the wrong time.

Speculation has a lot to do with timing. But for the sake of argument, I want to push the boundary and offer a less temporal and more fundamental view in line with putting dividends at the center of stock investing. The Random House dictionary lists a definition of *speculation* as "engagement in business transactions involving considerable risk but offering the chance of large gains, esp. trading in commodities, stocks, etc., in the hope of profit from changes in the market price." The last phrase is key. It is a matter of price, buyers and sellers, not the intrinsic worth sought by the likes of Williams, Keynes, and Graham. Measured against that definition, *all stocks without dividends are speculative*. Stocks like these are not necessarily dangerous or bad, but they are speculative in the narrow sense in that to realize value, a transaction has to occur. In Graham's day—he emerged on the scene in the 1930s—very few widely held securities did not have a dividend of some sort.

Today this type of speculation has taken on the much broader form of vast numbers of securities that don't have dividends at all. Witness the rise of the NASDAQ stock market during the 1980s and the 1990s where, as a general proposition, dividends are scarce, as opposed to the old-world, dividend-paying issues of the New York Stock Exchange (NYSE). Of the 3,770 U.S. stocks currently with a market value more than $50 million, 2,180 or 58% pay no dividend at all. Another 305 securities—including some of the largest businesses in this country—have a nominal payment amounting to a yield of less than 1.0%.[7] Taken together, the two groups represent just under two-thirds of all the U.S.-listed, common stocks in the market today and 42% of the market's capitalization. Over the past several decades, the United States has moved away from having a stock market where you got long-term cash streams in return for your capital in the direction of a trading market, a bazaar, where if you are lucky, you might get a penny here and there for holding onto your investments. Even among S&P 500 Index companies—the largest and generally most mature and dividend-oriented U.S. companies—the percentage of corporations paying a dividend has fallen in recent decades from 95% in 1965 to 72% in 2009.[8]

You might respond that there are many publicly traded stocks without dividends representing ownership interests in large, stable businesses—Warren Buffett's Berkshire-Hathaway is a good example—which themselves are hardly speculative. And you'd be right. That notion can be extended to an entire sector such as information technology. No one doubts the sector's overall profitability and durability, even if few of its publicly traded companies pay a significant dividend. Nevertheless, though individual businesses or even an entire sector might not be speculative, the stocks are if they have no dividend. Even if held for a long period of time, the nondividend payers still require a buyer and a transaction to generate *any* cash. I liken a stock without a dividend to a vintage baseball card. It can be fun to hold and looks good framed, but it only has cash value as part of a transaction. Unless you rent it out to the kid down the street, it does not generate any regular cash income, and to produce a positive return, it has to be sold for more than you paid for it. Earlier, I compared dividend investing to owning rental property. In its worst form, nondividend stock investing can also be like owning property. In this instance, however, the analogous property is a condominium in Las Vegas or on the west coast of Florida sometime during the past decade. Put down a preconstruction deposit, and start flipping to the next buyer. Whether the property is ever occupied or even gets built is immaterial. Like stock trading, that type of activity can be spectacularly profitable for a lucky and shrewd few, and reasonably profitable for many more, but we all know how it ends. The bubble bursts, and the last wave of buyers gets stuck with very expensive investments that they can sell only for a tremendous loss, if at all.

If you are uncomfortable imagining all of your non- or low-dividend paying holdings as speculative, you can turn this logic on its head and view them, theoretically, as a pure dividend investor might. Bear with me here for a moment as we make Google into a dividend stock. It may seem a stretch to argue that holders of Google are buying the stock for the dividend—it currently does not have one—but for Google to have any nonspeculative worth, we recall that there has to be a buyer out there who wants it for keeps, not to flip it. That buyer is implicitly assuming that at some point in the future, Google's board of directors will institute a dividend that will grow over time and that the value of those dividends discounted back to the present justifies today's $600 share price (as of October 2010). The dividend would presumably have to be very, very large and grow rapidly. Few if any current

Google shareholders view the situation in this light, but the mathematical rules of finance don't change just because people don't follow them. Instead, Google is being bought and sold in order to be bought and sold. That is . . . speculation.

But you will surely aver that the stock market isn't that bad. Most of the time people can "get out" with their cash, even if they are not the top-notch stock traders *cum* speculators. True, but two stock market crashes in the past decade— the tech bubble and then the financial crisis of 2008—suggest that stocks do not always go up and that they cannot always and immediately be "cashed out" for what they might have traded at in the past or what you think they might be worth. Those were exceptional moments in history, and let's hope that they don't return anytime soon. But what is more important is to realize that unless you are getting a cash stream from your stocks, you are entirely dependent for every last penny on someone buying them from you. That may not trouble you, but you ought to realize it just the same.

Dividends Dominate Total Return

My straw man definition of *speculation* can be easily dismissed as extreme, but its purpose is to emphasize how deeply trading in nondividend securities has become rooted in our nation's investing culture in recent decades, while dividend-based investing has been pushed into the background of our thinking. That is ironic because the point of investment is to make money. That is, the goal is not only to have a positive return, but to have as high a positive return as possible (also taking into account risk to the invested capital). You would think that as individuals and institutions set out to invest their hard-earned cash, they would focus, therefore, on what generates just those sorts of strong returns. Despite recurrent stock bubbles, manipulation, unavoidable daily price movements, outright frauds, and Ponzi schemes that can and do in the near term distort prices and returns from being a genuine reflection of business value, *dividends still dominate the components of total return.* (Total return in any given measurement period is the combination of the income received in the form of the dividend plus the change in the asset value—the stock price movement—both divided by the starting asset value.)

Conventional wisdom already has it that 40%–50% of the return from the market comes from dividends. You can run into that figure on the talk shows, in brokerage reports, on the Internet, in the works of stock market research firms. For instance, Ned Davis Research notes that 4.27% of the market's 9.73% return (44% of the total) from 1926 through 2009 came from dividends, with the rest, 5.46%, attributed to capital appreciation.[9] If you reach back to 1871 using Robert Shiller's database at Yale University, you can come up with a higher number: 4.7% of the 8.7% total return (or 54% of it) comes from the dividend yield and the rest from capital appreciation. The data is unambiguous. Whether looking at just the past 80 years or going further back, about half the return from equities in any given year comes directly from the dividend, and the rest from the stock movement. Just to get that "half," it would seem like a pretty good idea to focus your efforts on dividends. (These starting points, 1926 and 1871, are not random; they represent when different data sources began tracking the market. The S&P 500 Index came into being only in 1957. The other sources provide a glimpse into the pre–S&P 500 Index period.)

Although it is helpful, the conventional wisdom here is still wrong. In fact, closer to 90% of total returns from the stock market can be attributed directly to dividends. The 50% number is misleading in a way that reflects how in recent decades most investors have lost sight of what matters in the stock market. To appreciate the misdirection here, you have to understand how the financial services industry calculates performance. It consists of "period-linked" returns. That is, the primary calculation is done monthly, quarterly, or annually (a short period of time) and breaks down the total return for that period into an income component (the dividend) and the capital appreciation (how much the stock moved). Those period returns are then geometrically linked to cover long measurement periods, but they are still shown as the separate components of return in the much briefer period. When your financial advisor shows you a composite or a long-term return figure for an investment strategy, it is almost guaranteed to be a period-linked return based on short underlying timeframes. (The one very good reason for basing the calculation on short windows of time is that it takes out capital inflows and outflows that would throw off the intrinsic return measurement.)

Because period-linked returns cast short-term calculations as the basis for long-term returns, the quoted figures do not answer and in fact lead investors away from the quite simple but absolutely critical question: why did share prices go up by 5.5% annually since 1926? The answer is equally simple but not shown in the standard tables or charts: distributed profits have grown by that amount. Using Robert Shiller's data set, we can see that the market's aggregate dividend distribution has grown at a compound annual growth rate of 4.4% since 1926.[10] That is, of the market's annual total return of 9.7% since 1926, 8.6% of it (which amounts to 89% of the annual figure) came from dividends. The base dividend yield represented 4.2%, and the dividend growth subsequently reflected in capital appreciation provided 4.4%. Not a quarter, not a half, but almost 90% of the market's historical return has come from dividend payments. The difference between the market's overall return and the portions directly linked to the dividend is due to the fact that the yield of the market was 5.5% at the starting measurement and 2.0% at the end. In other words, between 1926 and 2009, the market became much more "expensive" (i.e., what people have been willing to pay for it has risen), but the growth in value independent of the dividend was just over 1% a year.

Going back further in time, the math is similar. Using the Shiller database from its starting point in 1871 through 2009, 91% of returns can be attributed to the dividend.[11] An analysis of returns for the past two centuries, from 1802 through 2002, puts the dividend component at 88%. During that time frame, U.S. equities averaged a return of 7.9% per year. Five percent (5.0%) came from the base dividend yield, 2.2% came from dividend growth, and only 0.7% (or 12% of the total) came from stock price appreciation independent of dividends.[12] Granted, the data from the early nineteenth century is highly selective and has been massaged, and dividend yields in the nineteenth century were much higher than in the twentieth, but the point is clear. Even in most recent decades, when payout ratios and dividend yields have plummeted, the component of total return represented by the dividend has remained high. Using rolling 10-year returns from 1970 to the present, Société Générale attributes 82.5% of U.S. market returns to dividend yield and dividend growth.[13]

This shouldn't come as a surprise. Over the long term, the value of companies increases primarily because distributable profits grow. Or to put it directly, *stocks go up because dividends go up*. It's not that complex or debatable. Why else would you want to own a stake in a company if not to access a growing stream of profits? And to be paid for it in cash? Dividends dominate the components of total return; invest in dividends.

Indeed, the longer the measurement period, the less important the small component represented by capital appreciation independent of dividend growth. In contrast, the way equity returns are typically presented—separate yield and capital appreciation figures—gives the impression that stocks move autonomously over the long term, that they are independent of distributable profit growth. That is simply not the case. In fact, over the long term, the stocks themselves are largely irrelevant. As John Burr Williams observed more than 70 years ago, "the longer a buyer holds a stock or bond, the more important are the dividends or coupons while he owns it and the less important is the price when he sells it. In the extreme case . . . the selling price in the end is a minor matter."[14]

That's why I want to introduce a counterintuitive concept that you will encounter repeatedly here: the key to successful stock investing is to take the stock out of the equation and to focus instead on what you actually receive from your invested capital. Yes, it is the case that now and in the past, people have bought and sold stocks for years at a time—and made or lost money in the process—without any regard to the dividends, dividend growth, or even the knowledge that by purchasing a stock they become partial owners of a company and are entitled to its distributable cash. But that reflection on human behavior doesn't change the basic mathematics of investment returns or the purpose of equities. While it is true that during a period like the 1990s it appeared that dividends had become irrelevant and stock prices were all that mattered, the following decade has showed quite the opposite. From the end of 1999 through the end of 2009, the S&P 500 Index fell by 24%. A decade of 2.0% and lower dividend yields brought the total return to a still disappointing decline of 9.0%, for an annual negative return of just less than 1.0%. Live by the sword . . . well, you know how it goes.

Though not top of mind for most investors now, long-term inflation is another critical reason to focus on dividends. The market's return figures are generally quoted in nominal terms. Take into account the impact of inflation, and the role of the dividend is even greater. That is because the basic dividend is received frequently and its contribution to total return is not subject to the reduction of purchasing power over time. It can be consumed at the time (e.g., food, rent, clothing) or reinvested so as to have more shares in an enterprise. In contrast, the capital appreciation portion of the equation is fully exposed to the impact of inflation. The real return in an equity investment is the amount by which the dividend grows faster than inflation (as well as any multiple expansion), plus the basic dividend yield received in the measurement period. Again using Robert Shiller's data set, we note that the market has returned 6.5% since 1926 in real terms, of which 4.2% came from the basic dividend yield and 2.3% came from real dividend growth (and capital appreciation independent of the dividend). The inflation-adjusted figure is a good deal less than most investors might imagine. The United States has enjoyed a declining and then outright low inflationary period since the early 1980s, and many investors, including professionals, have become used to quoting nominal returns without regard to inflation. It is one of the disturbing characteristics of our investment age and yet another reason to anchor your equity strategy around dividends.

The dominant role of the dividend is absolutely clear when one casually surveys the history of the stock market in this country, with the notable exception of the 25 years we have just gone through. Consistent with dividends dominating total returns, corporations paid out about half of their profits to their owners from the 1870s (as far back as we detailed data) for a century up through the 1970s. The payout ratio, as seen in Figure 1.1, did decline gradually in the postwar period but still remained between 40% and 60%.

FIGURE 1.1   S&P 500 Index Dividend Payout Ratio to 1982 (composite prior to 1957)

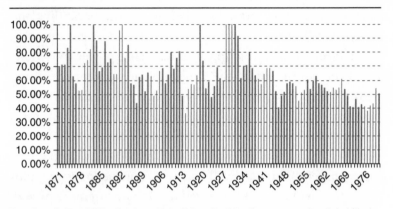

Data from Robert Shiller database, Yale University, http://www.econ.yale.edu/~shiller/data.htm.

The dividend yield of the market also varied over time but was in the 4.0%–6.0% range for most of that period (see Figure 1.2).

FIGURE 1.2   S&P 500 Index Dividend Yield to 1982 (composite prior to 1957)

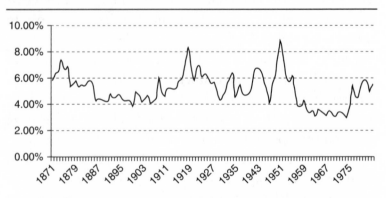

Data from Robert Shiller database, Yale University, http://www.econ.yale.edu/~shiller/data.htm.

Recall from our earlier review that a 4.0%–6.0% yield means 56% (4.0% capitalized at 14 times) to 84% (6.0% × 14) of the market's value at the time was captured by the present value of the dividend stream (using an arbitrary 7.0% discount rate). Growth in the income stream (about 4.4%) was able to generate an increase in the value of the market, not just to cover the market's cost.

In contrast, during the past 25 years, the market has changed dramatically. The amount that corporations paid out to company owners has fallen from 50% of profits to closer to 30%. The declining payouts and the willingness of investors to pay ever more for a modest income stream have pushed the market's yield to less than 2.0%. In effect, investors are no longer paying for the income stream at all. Few investors would want an annuity that pays less than 2.0% per year, even if the cash payment was expected to rise over time. Instead, those investors coming of age in the 1980s and 1990s were taught to seek out stocks that were going to go up, trade them, and repeat the process. No cash needed. Our grandparents, if they were fortunate enough to have the means to own equities, held stocks for the substantial dividend and for the dividend growth. If you have the opportunity, go ahead and ask them.

The popular understanding of equities in any period other than the recent past is equally clear. Whereas corporate managements currently use whatever trick they can to inflate earnings in the hope of boosting their share prices, in the nineteenth century Mark Twain cited "dividend cooking" as the means by which unscrupulous executives would try to achieve the same goal. In most cases, that meant simply paying dividends out of capital rather than profits. Why tamper with dividends? Because that's what investors looked at to measure the health of a company and to determine the proper share price! It's a simple story of horse and cart, still in the right order. Across the Atlantic, Karl Marx wrote in *Das Kapital* about English railroad companies falsifying their accounts to inflate their dividends.[15] U.S. railroad scandals very often involved the manipulation of dividends. The Crédit Mobilier affair that reached up into the White House of Ulysses S. Grant included dividend payments in cash and securities in 1868 that well exceeded 100% of the share price. Again, that is because dividends mattered. On Black Tuesday, October 29, 1929, the directors of two of the country's largest corporations at the time, U.S. Steel and American Can, did what they thought would steady the nerves of investors: they both declared special dividends of $1 per share. A few weeks later, General Motors also declared a special dividend. It did little good. That injection of cash could not overcome a decade of stock speculation. Go to the website of the original tech company, IBM (http://www.ibm.com/investor/financials). There you can find every dividend announced by the company going back to 1913. The stock prices are only available from 1980 and are provided from a third party.

In the 1960s, the market technician Edson Gould observed that the stock market tended to trade in a band between a 3% yield and a 6% yield, and could be viewed as overvalued or undervalued accordingly. (The market has been above the pricier end of the range for the better part of 20 years now.) Whether he was correct or not is less important to me than the fact that a leading student of the market focused on dividend yield as a primary measure of analysis. In 1991, Michael O'Higgins popularized an investment strategy—The Dogs of the Dow—based on the dividend yield of a subset of the Dow Jones Industrial Average securities. That is, as late as the early 1990s, dividends occupied a central position in the assessments of stocks. To paraphrase a vulgarity from the politics of the same period, "It's the dividend, stupid!" Indeed, as late as the last decade, major newspapers still published daily stock prices in their business sections. It may seem like ancient history, but reach back and recall what was actually listed in the eyesight-testing agate font. It was the name and the trailing 12-month dividend, as well as high, low, and closing prices for NYSE stocks. Ninety percent or so had them. The dividend mattered, even in a daily listing. For NASDAQ stocks, it was just name and price, with perhaps a smattering of over-the-counter listings offering a cash return to investors.

Even for the professional traders, knowing the dividend used to matter. I recently came across a photograph in a brokerage office in Oakland, California, that showed a scene from the Pacific Coast Stock Exchange in 1962. In the background on a large board were the NYSE listings being traded on the West Coast. The company names and annual dividends were in marquee letter tiles. They didn't change. On the ledge before the board stands a woman in Asian immigrant attire who writes on the board the ever-changing stock prices paid for ownership stakes in those companies and a claim on those dividends. What's a quaint anecdote worth? Not much. What's a lot of them worth? Not much more. Men also used to wear hats and women regularly wore long gloves. So what? Piling anecdote after anecdote about the importance of dividends is only useful to investors now if it is somehow relevant to how they might invest today. As we'll see, dividends have not lost their relevance for investors seeking to maximize returns.

The science of investment as it emerged in the early twentieth century also had dividends at the center of stock market analysis. The father of modern finance, Irving Fisher, wrote in 1906 that "the fundamental principle which applies here is that the value of capital at any instant is derived from the value of the future income which that capital is expected to yield. . . . Capital-value, independent of expected income, is impossible."[16] That goes for all investments, not just equities. Dividends from common stocks were the primary measure Edgar Lawrence Smith used in the 1920s to show that common stocks had bested bonds during the previous half century.[17] The dividend discount model (DDM)—a discounted cash flow model focusing on dividends—as we know it comes courtesy of John Burr Williams, whose *The Theory of Investment Value* (1938) made it perfectly clear that "a stock is worth the present value of all the dividends ever to be paid upon it, no more, no less. . . . Present earnings, outlook, financial condition, and capitalization should bear upon the price of a stock only as they assist buyers and sellers in estimating future dividends."[18] It can't get much simpler than that. The first significant how-to manual for stock analysts—Benjamin Graham and David Dodd's *Security Analysis* (1934)—also assumed that dividends were the primary component of long-term total return.[19] Suffice it here to observe that while fashions come and go, the intellectual founding fathers of modern investment analysis were quite certain of what was important and what was not. Seventy-five years later, notwithstanding recent "innovations" in popular thinking about how to determine the worth of a stock, the rules are still the same. One of the current age's leading writers on corporate valuation, Aswath Damodaran, states it clearly in his basic text: "When investors buy stock, they generally expect to get two types of cash flows: dividends during the period they hold the stock and an expected price at the end of the holding period. Since this expected price is itself determined by future dividends, the value of a stock is the present value of dividends through infinity."[20] Investors ignore these basic precepts at their own peril.

2

The Tortoise Beats the Hare, Again

High Yield and Dividend Growth

Now would probably be a good time to mention that on a total return basis, dividend-paying securities outperform non-dividend-paying ones, and that generally speaking, higher-dividend-yielding securities outperform lower-yielding ones. You would think that a book on investing would lead with this point, but to me it's almost unnecessary. In as much as dividends clearly dominate the components of total return over time, it's more of a confirmation that the system works rather than a statement of having found a clever new way to invest. Still, as we are in the midst (actually at the end) of a 25-year period when most company owners broke ranks with history and did not demand cash distributions from their investments, this fact is still worth pointing out and may come as a revelation to some. And it continues to be the case that over short periods of time, low-yielding stocks; nonyielding stocks; stocks less than $5; stocks that begin with the letters *B*, *H*, or *T*; or stocks based east of the Mississippi will outperform higher-yielding, dividend-growing stocks. And if you can trade those rotations successfully, then you will make a great deal of money quickly. But if you'd rather invest, look for dividend-paying, dividend-growing companies.

For illustration purposes, I've included two analyses from third parties. The first, Figure 2.1, from Ned Davis Research, Inc., looks at the S&P 500 Index returns since 1972 from a dividend perspective. The broad market benchmark is broken into dividend yield quartiles and one group for the non-dividend payers. The performance is measured monthly and then rebalanced. The result is pretty clear: the highest quartile does the best over time. Note how the non-dividend-paying stocks made a valiant charge during the tech boom in the 1990s before crashing in defeat. There was a lot of money to be made then (I recall a particular mania for Porsche Boxsters), but it was a garden-variety speculative bubble. Nothing more, nothing less.

FIGURE 2.1   S&P 500 Index Total Returns by Dividend Yield (1972 to 2009)

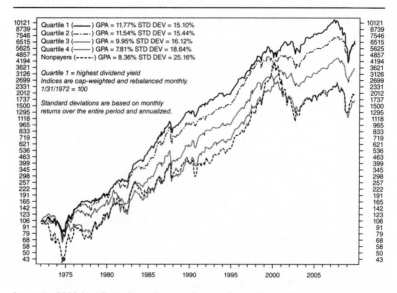

The second chart, Figure 2.2, goes back further to 1957 and comes courtesy of noted Wharton finance professor Jeremy Siegel. It shows the same thing: that the higher-yielding stocks outperform the lower-yielding ones. Both charts also include measures of volatility—beta and standard deviation—and both make the same point that the better results of the dividend stocks came with lower overall volatility. That makes sense when those securities have the benefit of a larger portion of their returns coming in cash payments, not the everyday swings of stock prices.

We're back in the world of period-linked returns, and it's important to highlight several shared characteristics of these performance numbers. First recall that in period-linked

FIGURE 2.2   S&P 500 Index Total Returns by Dividend Yield (1957 to 2009)

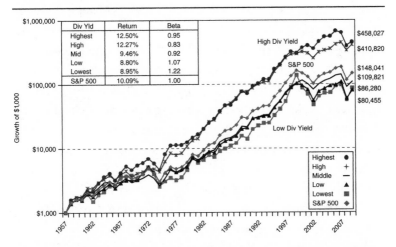

Source: Jeremy Siegel, data through 12/31/09. Each stock in S&P 500 Index is ranked from highest to lowest by dividend yield on December 31st of every year and placed into "quintiles," baskets of 100 stocks in each basket. The stocks in the quintiles are weighted by their market capitalization. The dividend yield is defined as each stock's annual dividends per share divided by its stock price as of December 31st of that year. Beta is a measurement of an index's trailing 36-month returns in relation to the appropriate market index.

returns, the income component and capital appreciation components are recorded separately for relatively short time frames—monthly in the first chart, annually in the second—and then used to create a return figure that is geometrically linked to next year's return figure. The result is the number in the upper left: about a 10% annual total return for the market, more for the higher-yielding securities and less for the lower-yielding ones. The figures on the right vertical axis show something quite different—an actual dollar value for an amount invested in each of the dividend buckets. Note that these so-called hypos (hypothetical investments) assume that all dividends are being reinvested. There's nothing wrong with that, but it does cast dividend investing in a somewhat different light in that the investors don't actually get the annual profit distributions from the companies owned. Similarly, the capital appreciation comes in part from simply getting more shares in the businesses through dividend reinvestment, not solely through the dividend increases in the companies eventually being reflected in their market prices. The alternative, dividends spun off, does not affect any individual period return—you get the same period-linked return indicated in the upper left-hand quarter of both charts—but it would lower the capital amounts shown on the right side. Tricky thing, these hypos. When you sit down with your consultant, make sure you understand the difference between period-linked compound annual growth rates and the beautiful charts showing astronomical performance of a $10,000 investment. They are not the same thing.

The second notable characteristic of these performance claims is that they reproduce the bias that the earlier data presentations do, but from the perspective of dividend yield. If the previous analyses breaking down total return into income and capital appreciation suggested that the latter occurred independently, these charts suggest that yield is the necessary and sufficient cause of outperformance. Not so. Think again how the stocks are divvied up. They are placed into quartiles or quintiles based on yield. And what happens when a company raises its dividend? The yield goes up. The stock finds itself in a higher-yielding subset, and over time, the market pushes the share price up and the yield back down. The more companies raise their dividends, the more the value of their businesses rise. While most of the securities in the higher-yielding buckets have raised their dividends over time, each group represents about a hundred or so stocks. There will always be some companies in the higher-yielding categories that have a notable yield but have not been able to increase their distributable profits and therefore their dividends. Those companies do not contribute to outperformance. To create an extreme example, if a company had the same dollar dividend now as it did in 1972 or 1957, it's not likely that it would be in that top-performing group of stocks. The stock would have moved sideways. Its annual total return would simply be its dividend yield, with no or little capital appreciation.

To address the bias in these charts, we need to view stock returns in a way that highlights the contributions of both yield and dividend growth to total return. The data in Table 2.1 comes from the returns of the 1,000 largest U.S. companies (by market capitalization) from 1970 through 2009. Note that the period includes the charge of the non-dividend payers in the 1990s and that the data set is large enough—1,000 companies rather than just the S&P 500—to include many of those smaller, non-dividend tech stocks everyone dreamed about owning in the 1990s. It is also equal weighted rather than market cap weighted, which provides another advantage to those small-cap tech names. Still, the results are quite stunning:

TABLE 2.1 Dividend Yield Plus Dividend Growth

		Universe	No Dividend	4th Quartile Yield (Lowest)	3rd Quartile Yield	2nd Quartile Yield	1st Quartile Yield (Highest)
Annualized Total Return (%)		10.77	8.19	9.82	11.04	12.83	12.24
Standard Deviation		19.83	29.32	21.04	19.08	17.60	18.50
Dividend Growth "Quintile"	High Growth	13.27		11.15	12.51	15.30	12.89
	Medium Growth	11.49		8.90	11.32	12.86	12.18
	Low Growth	10.27		8.85	9.42	10.85	11.25
	Flat Dividend	11.28		9.75	10.83	11.22	12.13
	No Dividend	8.19	8.19				

Largest 1,000 U.S. stocks; rebalanced annually; 12/31/1969–12/31/2009; equal-weighted returns. Data from FactSet Research Systems, 2010.

First of all, consistent with the previous third-party analyses and just about every review of historical return data ever conducted, dividend-paying stocks absolutely trounce the non-dividend payers, which returned just 8.19% over the measurement period, versus 10.77% for the broader universe. They do it with much lower volatility than the non-dividend securities, which bounce around a great deal without the anchor of a set dividend return. (The tech darlings of the 1990s became the tech disasters of the 2000s.) Generally speaking, the higher the yield, the better the return. That's the first row, moving to the right. Note that the highest-yielding column still outperformed the market but actually underperformed the second-highest-yielding silo. That's likely due to the fact that the highest-yielding group may include either pass-through securities (such as real estate investment trusts [REIT]) with little or no distribution growth or distressed companies that could not increase the dividend and perhaps even ultimately cut it or went out of business. Blindly reaching for extreme yield is not the best way to go for long-term total return. Similarly, securities that grew their distributions at higher rates showed higher total returns than companies that paid no dividend, kept it flat, or grew it slowly. Stocks go up because dividends go up. But the greatest return came from the combination of yield and growth, with three of the four top returning pairings being at the upper right of the matrix, at the intersection of the two highest yielding silos and the two fastest dividend growth buckets.

So let me summarize the key observations made here. Long-term total return is dominated by the dividend, by the combination of the basic yield and dividend growth. The capital appreciation component of total return is a consequence of dividend growth. Put the two together, and you have the formula for both a check in the mail from your ownership stake as well as a means of doing no worse and probably a good deal better than those trying to play the stock market. (Recall that whether or not the dividends are reinvested will not affect the period-linked returns but would of course alter the asset levels in your account.) Although not in these tables, it is still the case (I feel I have to mention this every few pages) that in any given month, quarter, or even a several-year period, dividends can be utterly irrelevant. Buyers and sellers of stocks can be occupied by other matters, caught up in bubbles, or sell down good dividend-paying securities for any reason. But over the long term, the combination of dividend yield and dividend growth drives stock market returns.

So far, so good, you may say. But 40 years (not to mention a century or two) is a long time to wait for a particular investment strategy to bear fruit. Many investors claim that they are investing for the long term, but four decades is asking too much of most retail and every institutional money manager. What about shorter time periods? The marketplace reality is that the combination of daily liquidity (the ability to sell stocks at will) and human impatience make it hard for investors, particularly retail investors, to hold on to a product that isn't "working" *now*, defined as the last 12 months, or for some really impatient investors, even the last few weeks. Those investors are doing themselves a tremendous disservice. I've already mentioned the studies that show that most mutual funds do much better over longer measurement periods than the investors who move in and out of them for shorter periods of time. That is because the mutual fund investors are impatient and sell when they should be buying or holding on, or they are excessively confident after a good run and linger when they should sell.

How does dividend investing work in shorter time frames? Remarkably well. We've taken the same data set behind the

40-year, total return analysis just presented and created a series of rolling 10-, 5-, and 3-year measurement periods. In each one, the annual total return of the two highest dividend-yielding quintiles is measured against the two lowest-yielding buckets. The annualized difference between high and low for each rolling period is shown as a column. A positive number indicates that the higher-dividend securities did better.

For the 10-year period, the outcome (shown in Figure 2.3) is as expected. Higher yield outperforms lower and no yield just about every period and does so by about 3.0% annually.

The 5-year measurement window (see Figure 2.4) is not much different. Inflation in the late 1970s and early 1980s took its toll, as did the recession of the early 1990s followed by the tech bubble, but most of the columns have positive values. The average measure of annual outperformance was 1.5%.

FIGURE 2.3   Rolling 10-Year High Yield Versus Low/No Yield, Annualized Return (1970 through 2009)

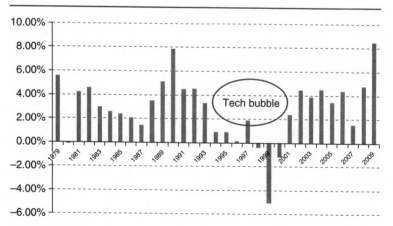

Largest 1,000 U.S. stocks, equal weighted, rebalanced annually. Data from FactSet Research Systems, 2010.

FIGURE 2.4   Rolling 5-Year High Yield Versus Low/No Yield, Annualized Return (1970 through 2009)

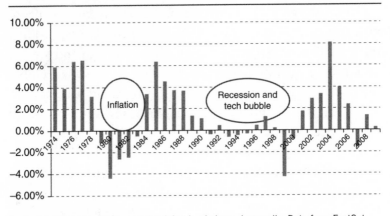

Largest 1,000 U.S. stocks, equal weighted, rebalanced annually. Data from FactSet Research Systems, 2010.

Perhaps the most interesting result, however, is for the rolling 3-year period (see Figure 2.5). From a dividend-investing perspective, this is the equivalent of a sprint, and it is one in which we would expect the hare to do as well as the tortoise.

For the shorter periods, you do see much greater economic sensitivity. The economic challenges of the late 1970s and early 1980s hurt dividend-yielding securities as did the recession of the early 1990s and the final throes of the tech bubble. The record over the past decade has been choppy: behind in 2007, ahead in 2008, behind in 2009. Still, the Yankees don't win every game, just most of them, and by the end of the season, they are usually ahead. That's what matters. In two-thirds of the three-year measurement periods (24 out of 38), the higher-yielding securities did better than the low- and no-yielding ones, with an average outperformance of just less than 1.0% per year. While it's good to know that dividend investing outperforms the alternative much of the time, the key thing for investors to do is to reject judging their portfo-

FIGURE 2.5 Rolling 3-Year High Yield Versus Low/No Yield, Annualized Return (1970 through 2009)

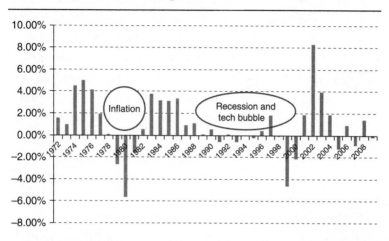

Largest 1,000 U.S. stocks, equal weighted, rebalanced annually. Data from FactSet Research Systems, 2010.

lios over short time periods. For most investors, short-term decision making is the formula for guaranteed long-term underperformance.

In Chapter 1, we reviewed how the math of present value calculations strongly favors higher-yielding equities. The goal should be to cover as much as possible of the purchase price with the current income stream, leaving dividend growth to cover the rest and provide for capital appreciation. Here we've seen how studies of broad market returns using 500 or 1,000 stocks reset every year, sliced and diced in every possible way, also favor portfolios of higher-yielding, dividend-growing securities. Both are important assertions in favor of tapping into dividend streams as your key investment objective, but neither is directly relevant to how typical investors experience the market. While you can and should take comfort in the mathematics of present value calculations, buying stocks does not take place in a controlled, laboratory environment, and you will not likely find an individual stock that year in and year out generates a 5.0% cash return and goes up by 5.0% per year reflecting an increase in the dividend of the same amount. At the other end of the impractical spectrum, broad studies of stock market returns would have you own hundreds of stocks and trade them frequently to get the desired results. These exercises generally do not take into account transaction costs, which can be substantial, and therefore they may overstate your expected return. More generally, data analyses are necessarily backward looking. They may provide a good indication of what will happen in the future, but they can never predict it exactly.

In the real world, the goal is to have a manageably sized portfolio of 40 to 60 dividend streams (stocks) that combines the attributes of high current yield and some measure of dividend growth. That generally means choosing stocks from the highest- and second-highest-yielding buckets that can not only maintain their distributions but also grow them at least modestly over the next five years. (Presumably the companies can grow them for longer than that, but you don't want to try to predict business conditions much beyond five years out.) This strategy draws on the power of the present value calculations as well as the past record of dividend-focused securities in the stock market, without being a slave to either approach. If you project this approach back into the past, how would it have done over time? Quite well, as you might expect. If over the past 30 years, you took a portfolio of the 50 highest-yielding stocks (from a universe of the 500 largest securities at the time) that also showed a past record of dividend increases and some ability to raise their dividends in the future (the tricky part), it grew at a rate of 14.66% versus the universe return of 11.25%. It also showed a standard deviation (a measure of volatility) of 14.51% versus the universe's 17.73%.[1] This is still a backward-looking exercise, and past performance is no guarantee of future results, but it is yet another submission, Ladies and Gentlemen of the jury, that *dividends dominate the components of total return, so invest in dividends.*

Cause or Effect?

Correlation does not equal causality, as many of my analyst friends would note at this point. In other words, the fact that dividends are associated with strong stock returns does not prove that the dividends cause the outperformance. True, but it is also the case that this strong a relationship over such a long period of time—well documented at least as far back as 1871—makes one feel more comfortable with the assertion. Also, the nature of discounted cash flow or dividend discount models that posit the worth of a security as the present value of its future cash payments hints strongly at causality. Still, is there something else *within* the stock market that we are missing? I don't think so. To my mind, stepping *outside* the stock market to the analysis of business practices does uncover the causes behind the strong showing of dividend-oriented securities, and it is consistent with seeing the market as a means to another end, not a speculative end unto itself. It is twofold and a repetition of what we've already stated.

The first cause is obvious: the growth of company profits that permits an increase in the distributions to owners of the company. In finance, it is the return generated from incremental capital. In the real world it is a matter of business acumen, application, and a little luck. Saying it is simple; achieving it is the task of much of the adult population working in the private sector. The second, less intuitive but perhaps more powerful, cause is the distribution of excess profits to owners of a company, rather than a company's other use of them. This distribution contributes the base yield that is such an important component of total return. The explanation of why a higher distribution propels superior total return is relatively straightforward. You have to have a healthy dividend payout to have a substantial dividend yield. Without a dividend, or with an inconsequential one from a mature company, you miss out on much of the total return that can be expected from an equity investment. As we've demonstrated earlier, companies with payouts and at least some yield do far better than those without. But what is notable when looking at stock returns over the past 40 years, as shown in Table 2.2, is that they do not diminish materially as you move up the payout scale. In fact, the returns are largely bunched together.

This seems to fly in the face of the commonsense observation that greater reinvestment leads to greater growth. I take no great pleasure in casting doubt on the virtues of reinvesting profits in a business. It is absolutely critical to the growth of enterprises and to our society as a whole. Unfortunately, it is hard to tell which investments work well and which don't. Real life is not a laboratory; you can't run a controlled experiment. I've heard former General Electric CEO Jack Welch (and others) quip that half of the decisions he made were wrong. He just didn't know which half. The reality is that investors are better off taking the cash than leaving more than is necessary in the hands of managers. Some companies

TABLE 2.2   Dividend Payout Ratios and Total Return

	No Dividend	Low Payout	3rd Payout	2nd Payout	High Payout
Annualized Total Return (%)	8.19	11.63	11.84	11.33	11.27
Standard Deviation	29.32	21.74	19.03	16.74	17.71

Largest 1,000 U.S. stocks; rebalanced annually; 12/31/1969–12/31/2009; equal-weighted returns. Data from FactSet Research Systems, 2010.

may be able to grow their dividends consistently at a higher rate with a lower payout, but from a total return perspective, that gain is essentially entirely offset by the higher cash component of return coming from the higher-payout companies. Or to put it another way, companies that pay their owners more rather than less of the profits do not suffer lower total returns, in large part because of those payments.[2] And by returning the excess profits to shareholders as a cash payment, it is an absolute form of return. There is no stock market involved in the process to call into question the value of the dividend. Cash is cash.

The key seems to be the discipline of the payout. It makes managers much less likely to put money into unnecessary projects and to manage costs closely. It also constrains the opportunity to pursue large acquisitions (they usually fail) and wasteful share repurchases, a topic we will review later. At the outset of this book, I likened dividend investing to how someone might run his or her own business. The practicalities of large-scale investment dictate, however, that client money be put into companies where we are not the manager-owner, just the owner. That greater scale comes at the cost of a conflict of interest because it is the rare CEO who is not tempted to reinvest most of his or her company's profits to build a business empire. A low payout facilitates that tendency. A high payout doesn't get rid of the temptation, but it does make CEOs much more circumspect. "Paying out a dividend does not guarantee great results, but it does improve the return of the typical stock by yanking at least some cash out of the manager's hands before they can either squander it or squirrel it away."[3] Even fewer CEOs appreciate that it is the payout, not the high reinvestment rate, that generates long-term total return. Try telling one of them (as I did on a recent investor trip to Toronto to meet bank executives) that the best strategy from an investor perspective was to scale back the bank's potentially expensive plans to take share in the already mature, stable Canadian financial sector and simply to focus on generating and distributing the profits inherent in the commercial banking model. The executive laughed and said that if he went to his board of directors and told them that the best way to maximize shareholder return might well be to do nothing, he would soon have plenty of time to improve his golf game.

It would be career suicide to opt in favor of paying out profits to investors. Still, the market bears out the observation that having to subordinate one's capital allocation process to the discipline of a high cash payout to company owners is a good idea. Low payout ratios justified by the claim that the profits held back will be reinvested to generate greater profits and dividends in the future ignore not only the possibility that the investments might fail, but the absolute certainty that those future dividend payments will have to be discounted. In short, a low payout ratio at a large, mature firm is a nice luxury for a competent management team and an absolute necessity for a less talented one.

I wish it were as simple as suggesting that a higher payout leads to better long-term returns due to the constraints that it puts on senior managers. The reality is more complex because companies are cyclical in their performance, and the calculations that show the benefits of higher payouts may incorporate that cyclicality. Start the measurement period near the low point of the business cycle, and the company's payout and yield appear to be high. Mean reversion does the rest, and the next 10 years look great from an earnings, dividend growth, and total return perspective. Start near the top of the cycle, and the opposite is the case. The truth is somewhere in between. While company cyclicality effectively precludes making the claim that a higher payout ratio always leads to significant stock outperformance versus that of lower-payout companies, that same cyclicality does not invalidate the role played in total return by the base dividend yield itself. And generally speaking, the higher the payout, the higher the yield for investors.

Dividends and dividend growth are not the cause of successful investing; they are the manifestation of it, of the growth and distribution of company profits. Dividend stocks outperform alternative stock strategies in the long run because they are best aligned with the underlying purpose of most public equity investments: the distribution of excess profits to owners of modestly growing, usually mature companies. Let me be clear: there is plenty of room in the stock market for non-dividend-paying companies raising capital and reinvesting all of their profits (if they have them), but it is a matter of scale. They should not dominate the market as they have come to in recent decades. That makes, or shall I say made, the market into a casino.

Reynolds American: A Case Study in Low Growth, High Payout, and Spectacular Total Return

Table 2.3 illustrates my point about payouts and growth with an extreme example, one in which a high payout ratio from a company in a *declining* industry did not prevent it from delivering superior dividend growth and investment returns. Consider the maker of Camel cigarettes: Reynolds American Inc. (RAI) started trading as an independent tobacco company (under the name R. J. Reynolds Tobacco Holdings, Inc.) on June 15, 1999, and closed that day at $16.22 per share on a split-adjusted basis. (The century-old Reynolds tobacco business had spent the 1980s and 1990s as part of a larger conglomerate known as RJR Nabisco, Inc.) The next month, the new entity declared its first quarterly dividend of $0.3875 cents per share. In the following analysis, I've captured the stock and dividend information about Reynolds from 2000 through the end of 2009.

TABLE 2.3 Reynolds American (RAI)

	Annual Dividend	Reported EPS	Operating EPS	Operating Payout	Share Price Beginning of Period	Share Price End of Period	Price Return	Dividend Return	Simple Total Return	Index Return 100	Cigarettes Made (Billions)
1999–2000	$1.55	$8.97	$1.99	77.9%	$16.22	$24.38	50.3%	9.6%	59.8%	159.8	145.6
2001	$1.65	$2.20	$2.24	73.7%	$24.38	$28.15	15.5%	6.8%	22.3%	195.4	135.2
2002	$1.86	($0.25)	$3.11	59.8%	$28.15	$21.06	−25.2%	6.6%	−18.6%	159.1	135.3
2003	$1.90	($20.59)	$3.34	56.9%	$21.06	$29.08	38.1%	9.0%	47.1%	234.0	120.3
2004	$1.90	$3.09	$3.86	49.2%	$29.08	$39.30	35.2%	6.5%	41.7%	331.6	118.2
2005	$2.10	$3.53	$4.04	52.0%	$39.30	$47.67	21.3%	5.3%	26.6%	419.9	107.4
2006	$2.75	$4.10	$4.14	66.4%	$47.67	$65.47	37.4%	5.8%	43.1%	601.0	104.0
2007	$3.20	$4.43	$4.61	69.4%	$65.47	$65.96	0.7%	4.9%	5.6%	634.8	97.8
2008	$3.40	$4.57	$4.73	71.9%	$65.96	$40.31	−38.9%	5.2%	−33.7%	420.7	89.5
2009	$3.60	$3.30	$4.64	77.6%	$40.31	$52.97	31.4%	8.9%	40.3%	590.4	81.7
CAGR	9.8%			Median	67.9%	CAGR	12.6%		CAGR	19.4%	−6.2%
Total	$23.91			Aggregate	65.1%	Total	226.6%		Total	490.4%	−43.9%

RAI shares ended 1999 at a particularly depressed share price of $8.81. Using that as the starting share price would have artificially raised price and dividend returns. Instead, the closing price on June 15, the day of issue, is used. The other 1999–2000 operating figures are from calendar year 2000. Data from FactSet Research Systems, 2010, and Morgan Stanley.

Throughout this period, the number of cigarettes sold in this country continued its long-term decline of 3.0%–4.0% per year, a trend that we as citizens should applaud. Reynolds has seen its own "stick" count decline by more than 6.0% per year during the past decade. As a result of its secular decline, the industry has continued to consolidate and to cut costs. In 2004, Reynolds, the country's number two cigarette maker, combined with Brown & Williamson, the number three vendor. It also moved into the smokeless tobacco category by acquisition. Though the industry has become much smaller over the past decade, RAI has been able to grow its annual dividend consistently at a rate of around 10% per year. It is now more than twice what it was a decade ago. And it grew the dividend while still maintaining a very high payout by U.S. industry standards of roughly two-thirds of operating profits.

In the interim, the share price of Reynolds stock has been very volatile. It was knocked about by the Master Settlement Agreement of 1998 that imposed huge new taxes on smokers; a massive federal racketeering lawsuit announced in late September 1999, soon after RAI had resumed trading; a recession in 2001–2002; and the overall legal challenges that periodically threaten to bankrupt the industry.[4] (Reynolds is the exception that proves the rule that high-dividend-yielding investments are less volatile than lower-yielding ones.) While those were valid concerns for dividend investors—as they could have affected cash flows dramatically—the diligent analyst could have asserted that the recession was temporary and that the legal challenges would be overcome, as they were. In the meantime, the cash flow on a per-share basis continued to grow steadily. Even after adjusting the starting price of the measurement period to account for the near-term impact of the government's lawsuit (which pushed the RAI share price down 50% between June 1999 and the end of the year) so that the results would not be overstated, the total return generated by the high annual payment and the growth of that payment is phenomenal. In contrast, the S&P 500 Index has lost ground in this period, with the market's skimpy annual dividend yield of less than 2.0% only partially offsetting a 24% decline in price.

An investment in RAI highlights the difference between playing the stock market to find the next big thing and investing through the stock market to increase wealth. They are not the same. In fact, they often are quite the opposite. You don't necessarily need a rapid growth industry to generate stellar returns. Expectations are so high around emerging technologies, for instance, that it is very hard to generate a competitive stock return in them versus an investment in a more moderately priced (higher yielding) security in a more mature industry. With the exception of perhaps Google or eBay—discussed later—you'll be hard pressed to find more than a handful of technology or Internet companies with stock results over the past decade that come close to equaling those generated by the cigarette companies. That's one of the most common misconceptions about the stock market—confusing the company and the investment.

Owning the Apple Computer company's products because they are stylish and intelligently designed should not be conflated with the goal of making money out of an investment in Apple's stock. These are entirely different purposes and require a different analytical process. Similarly, you don't have to embrace or have even a positive long-term outlook on a declining industry, such as cigarettes, to come to the conclusion that it might make a great investment. To wit, let me end this section by comparing an investment in Apple Computer versus one in a cigarette company.

Apple Computer Versus Altria

Apple's shares were originally sold to the public in late 1980. The only cigarette company trading at that time and still trading today is MO, currently called Altria but at the time known as Philip Morris Companies, Inc. In the 1980s, Altria was a conglomerate including Kraft, General Foods, and Miller Beer, among other divisions. Generally speaking, Altria has been a slow-growing company in mature sectors of the economy. Apple has been quite the opposite. The stock returns since Apple's launch through the end of 2009 are shown in Table 2.4. The nearly 500-basis-point difference in annual return in favor of Marlboro, Kraft Macaroni & Cheese, and Miller Genuine Draft—all steadily declining businesses—makes quite clear the difference between an investment in a growth company and an investment that grows in value. The quintessential hare, Apple Computer, is ahead on price appreciation, but cannot possibly keep up with Altria once the dividend payments are thrown into the equation.

Critics here will point out the gross "survivorship bias" (i.e., incorporating the results of only the companies that exist throughout the entire measurement period) in using Altria as the single tobacco stock trading then and now. They are correct. But the survivorship bias in choosing Apple for the technology issue would be vastly greater. The investment roadside

TABLE 2.4   Apple Computer (APPL) Versus Altria (MO), 1981–2009

	Price Return (%)	Total Return (%)	CAGR (%)
AAPL	4,831	5,303	14.75
MO	4,555	17,696	19.56

Returns from 12/31/1980 to 12/31/2009. Data from Sanford C. Bernstein & Co., LLC, and Federated Investors, Inc., 2010.

is littered with the corpses of hundreds if not thousands of technology hares. All the while, the tortoises trundle on. Using an index that captures the fates of the technology and tobacco securities that were trading in each annual measurement period does not entirely account for survivorship bias, but it goes a long way toward offsetting it. And the results are the same. Comparing the returns of the NASDAQ-100 Index and the S&P 500 Tobacco Index from 1993 through 2009 (as far back as there is detailed data) in Table 2.5 once again shows the tortoise leaving the hare far behind, even in a period of unparalleled decline for one industry and growth for the other.

TABLE 2.5   S&P 500 Tobacco Index Versus NASDAQ-100 Index, 1993–2009

	Price Return (%)	Total Return (%)	CAGR (%)
NASDAQ-100 Index	416	444	10.5
S&P 500 Tobacco Index	243	644	12.5

Data from Bloomberg, LLP, 2010.

Indeed, the NASDAQ stocks "went up" more than the stocks of the cigarette companies, but when the dividend is included, the tobacco companies generated total returns that were on average 2.0% per year greater than the tech names.

What About the Alternatives?

The evidence in favor of dividends is overwhelming—the power of present value calculations, the role of dividends in the stock market's history, the lopsided performance vis-à-vis non- or low-dividend-paying securities—but could the focus on dividends still be misguided? Over the years, investors have sought to master the market in a variety of ways. To the extent that they could be viewed as alternatives to dividend investing, they are reviewed here briefly.

Value Investing

The most obvious alternative to dividend investing is the broader notion of value investing. Academic observers have suggested that a dividend strategy is, in fact, simply a subset of the larger value approach to the market. Technically they are correct. Almost all dividend-oriented equities fall into the category of value stocks. Distinguished from growth stocks, value stocks are those securities that are in the less-expensive half of the stock market as determined by a variety of typical measures such as price-to-sales (P/S), price-to-book value (P/B), and price-to-earnings (P/E). It is also true that over longer measurement periods, value outperforms growth and the broader market. (During the growth-dominated 1990s that "virtue" would have been hard to appreciate.) Some of the most notable investors in the recent, nondividend age have made their fame and fortune as value managers by identifying companies trading below what they consider to be an intrinsic value, regardless of whether or not there is dividend in the equation. One very important shared trait between value investing and dividend investing is the holding period. Value investors are not traders, and for that we salute them. Though not necessarily anchored to a dividend the way we choose to be, they are investing for the long term and doing so on the basis of business analysis, not the everyday reading of the market's entrails that has come to pass for stock investing.

So perhaps dividends are just coincidental with a more powerful underlying factor? That could be, but there are several very important distinguishing characteristics between value and dividend securities that should lead one to stay close to the dividend subset.

First, the dividend is absolute; value is relative. In more normal times (higher payouts, higher yields), the overlap of dividend and value characteristics in the stock market would be greater. In the present environment, however, they are not.

Second, while essentially all dividend securities are considered value stocks, it is not the other way around. Indeed, much of the value universe is indifferent to dividends. The yields of the leading value indices are not much higher than the yield of the overall market. Many value companies have low payout ratios, a low yield, and little or no commitment to distribute profits to the owners of the company. Some "deep" value stocks have no dividend at all, because they don't have profits to distribute. That is not to say that there isn't genuine intrinsic "value" in many stocks in the bottom half of the valuation lists. The financial crisis of 2008 provided many good examples where some leading, well-run institutions were temporarily stripped of their profits and dividends and saw their share prices pushed down to levels suggesting bankruptcy. For those investors who did their homework, these stocks represented great, if speculative, opportunities. Whether encountered during a crisis or more normal times, securities like these have a role to play for investors, and some clients have asked us why we do not buy bank (and consumer discretionary or industrial) value stocks in expectation of dividends being reinstituted at some point in the future. Our answer is that when that blessed event happens, we'll take a look at them. In the meantime, we can't deliver a dividend check to our clients if we don't receive one from our companies. What if it is years before the dividends are reinstated or if they are just a nominal nickel payment each quarter? That's not for us. Instead, for us the value of an investment is intrinsically tied to the ability to receive a cash return and to do so when we enter the relationship. The strategy is not bold, but it is a disciplined approach to investing that goes a long way to keeping clients out of value "traps," companies that cannot increase or distribute their profits for many years and as a result do not grow in worth.

In addition, before assessing whether value might constitute a better analytical framework for investing than dividends, it would be good to have a definition of value that we can use over time. Beyond being relative rather than absolute in nature, the notion of value itself has become hard to define in recent decades. Both P/E and P/B have largely been polluted by modern conventions—earnings not in accordance with GAAP (generally accepted accounting principles) and all manner of adjustments to book value—that inflate a company's supposed relative value by pushing up the denominator. Having realized that P/E and P/B are no longer particularly useful, many value investors have started to shift their focus from company income statements and balance sheets to the cash flow statement to answer the basic question of how much cash a company is generating and what investors are paying for that cash.

While it is the case that cash flow statements can be misleading and manipulated by management's near-term actions, as a rule they have not yet been as abused as the other two views. I'll have more on financial statement analysis later, but let me briefly introduce here free cash flow (FCF) as cash flow from operations minus capital expenditures. In a steady-state business and taking into account depreciation, capital expenditures, and working capital, FCF per share should be about the same as EPS (earnings per share) were the latter accurately reported. As it often is not, FCF per share can measure by how much the company is really covering its dividend. Unable to recommend stocks on the basis of high dividend yield, Wall Street brokerages have shifted to trying to sell stocks to value investors on the basis of a high FCF yield—the FCF per share divided by the share price. The problem with FCF yield is that it is too often assumed to be free cash flow to the shareholders when it is in fact free cash flow to company management who can use it as they see fit. (In contrast, the dividend yield is what the investor actually gets.) The sell-side analysts working for the brokerages and many of their value-oriented clients are indifferent as to whether the free cash is used to pay the dividend, buy up other companies, or repurchase shares. As dividend investors, we are not indifferent, nor should you be. Large acquisitions fail more often than not, and share repurchase programs, as we will see, are a very bad idea. Suffice it to say here, equating "firm yield" (as it has been called) with shareholder or dividend yield tries to make a virtue of necessity. Do not be fooled. You became a company owner to get a cash return, not for some other fellow to have discretion over your cash.

Finally, without the anchor of a notable dividend yield, value stocks look and trade like, well, stocks. Most, if not all, of the return to the owner has to come from selling the security to someone for more than the purchase price. Unless you are a disciplined, very patient investor, that means playing or at least enduring the Wall Street game of earnings "surprises," multiple expansion and contraction, sector rotation, as well as getting "in" and "out" in a timely fashion. Investing in value stocks may be easier than riding the roller coaster of growth stocks, but in its modern variant, value investing is still a market strategy with only a minimal cash component and a reliance on Wall Street. Rather than dismiss all of value investing (because there is much to recommend it), I would offer the view that dividends are the tangible expression of a successful value approach that has necessarily become narrower in the past several decades as dividends have become a smaller and smaller subset of the value world. Whereas before the 1980s, value and dividend investing would have largely overlapped in theory and practice, dividend investing is now value investing focused on receiving cash payments.

Before leaving value investing, I want to circle back to its high priest, Benjamin Graham. His book *The Intelligent Investor* (1949) and his earlier work with David Dodd, *Security Analysis* (1934), together constitute the Holy Scripture of value investing. And like the Bible, they are more often quoted than actually read. The legacy of Graham and Dodd has been further confused because their leading contemporary interpreter, Warren Buffett, has downplayed dividends and said that investors don't care that much about them. His own investment vehicle, Berkshire-Hathaway, has not paid a dividend in more than 40 years. But Buffett's public indifference to dividends is belied by his actions. In recent decades he has bought entire companies. That is, *all* of the excess cash flow belongs to Berkshire-Hathaway. And many of his minority investments in publicly traded companies have been in firms with notable dividend yields.

Nevertheless, the Oracle of Omaha's stance on dividends has come to be taken as a direct expression of Graham and Dodd. I recommend that you go back to the original source. Benjamin Graham's canon is strongly rooted in dividends, perhaps not as stridently as argued here, but to a much greater degree than the current industry of value investing, which assigns little, if any, significance to them. In Graham's time, value investing and dividend investing were more or less the same thing. Indulge me with a few extended quotes about investing and dividends from Graham and Dodd:

The outside, or public, stockholder gets no tangible, realizable benefits from his investment except by way of dividends received thereon or through an increase in the market price. The latter in turn is usually dependent upon the former. Assuming indefi-

nite continuance of the business, the theoretical importance of earnings is confined to their effect on dividends, either current or future. To make an extreme case, if the outside investor knew that a profitable business was never going to pay a dividend and was never going to be sold out or dissolved, the value of the stock to him would be virtually nil. Thus, it is an accepted tenet of financial theory that the present value of any preferred or common stock issue, and any other investment assumed to have no maturity or repayment date for its principal, is the sum of the (discounted) present values of all the future expectable dividends or interest payments therefrom.[5]

Dividends were basically the most important single factor in valuation from the standpoint of the ordinary public stockholder; that earnings were chiefly important because of their bearing on present and future dividends; and that average market prices were influenced (and properly so) to a preponderant degree by the company's payout policy. If these views are correct, their implications for stockholders are obvious. They should insist on adequate dividends. They should not accept banal and unconvincing explanations of failure to pay adequate dividends. They should support efforts by fellow stockholders to persuade or compel management to adopt an adequate dividend rate.[6]

Times have changed since the 1930s and 1940s when *Security Analysis* and *The Intelligent Investor* initially appeared. (Both were subsequently revised and reissued into the early 1970s.) Not all the lessons still apply, but the main ones do. With all due respect to the Oracle of Omaha, if you as an investor claim to believe in Graham and Dodd, go back and read the original text to appreciate the role accorded to dividends.

Growth Investing

If not value investing as it has come to be defined today, could its "opposite," growth investing, hold the key to understanding the role of dividends in stock market performance? One obvious objection to the framework outlined in this book is that I'm drawing a distinction between dividend growth and garden variety "earnings growth" chased by everyone on Wall Street. Aren't they the same? Certainly not, but you are forgiven in the age of Internet stocks for asking that question. The first part of the answer is that the basic dividend yield is such a large component of total return over time from equities that to forego it entirely to focus on capital appreciation via "growth" all but guarantees subpar returns. If a company has substantial earnings but does not pay much of them out, there is something wrong. Enough said.

The second part of the answer is that it is incredibly hard to find companies that have increased their distributable profits over the years and have not raised their dividend to suit (I know of none). Do you know of any major American or global corporations that have been around for decades and are trading with 0.1% yields because they never raised their distributions in line with profits? (The banks and other institutions that now sport 0.1% yields do so because they cut their previously high dividends.) A dividend is a commitment to pay the owners of the company a cash return on their investment. Large, well-established companies simply do not sit on their excess profits. They distribute them to the owners of the company. If they do not, the owners sell their stakes. That drives the price down to a level where the incremental investors would be getting an appropriate cash return for their money. For stocks with no or very low dividends, there is no such floor, no such "guaranteed" return.

Over the long term, of course, profit growth and dividend growth have to be in line with one another (assuming a constant payout ratio), and before the accounting and stock market innovations of the past few decades, I would have felt comfortable using the terms interchangeably. But not anymore. Wall Street has a 12-month time horizon at best for profit growth, and companies and Wall Street analysts are now willing to employ all the tricks of the trade to show their near-term earnings numbers in a positive light. As a result, the notion of EPS growth has become so debased that it really is a useless measure of long-term profit and dividend trajectories. For long-term investors, dividend growth is real earnings growth. As a cash payment, the dividend can't be faked (though it can be borrowed) and is not subject to non-GAAP adjustments.

You might then rightly point to the need for small, early-stage companies to reinvest profits to further their expansion. I'm not denying the importance of profit reinvestment and that high-growth businesses will and should have low payout ratios or even zero payouts for many years. But at a certain point you can have too many early-stage companies raising too much capital in the public equity markets, investing way too much in failed projects (e.g., remember all that fiber-optic cable in the 1990s), merging and acquiring one another at ridiculous valuations, or using their capital to buy back their shares at inflated prices. In retrospect, it's perfectly clear that many of those tech darlings that issued stock to the public in the 1990s should have remained funded by venture capital and private equity, both of which are designed to take on early-stage, loss-making, high-risk investments that either go bust or work out spectacularly. That is not to say there is not room in the public equity markets for loss-making, early-stage enterprises. But during the tech craze, they flooded Wall Street and main street brokerage accounts and contributed to the alternate, (mis)understanding of the role of the public equity markets.

You may then point out the growth success stories of Microsoft, Amazon, eBay, and Google. Keep in mind that these companies are one in a thousand or ten thousand, and the jury is still out as to whether these survivors will eventually become dividend-oriented. Microsoft is arguably a mature company that has excess, distributable profits. About a decade ago, it started paying a dividend. Then in 2004 it paid a very hefty special dividend of $3.00 per share to lighten its load of excess cash. (The market's reaction was generally negative; it was the wrong audience.) It has been steadily increasing its distributions to its owners in line with or even better than its reported earnings growth. Although the return pattern is not yet fully skewed toward the dividend, Microsoft is moving in that direction.

An even older company, Intel, is already there. It long ago shifted toward paying shareholders in cash. Its dividend yield—3.0% at time of writing—is very high for a tech stock, and Intel has been steadily raising its cash distributions to company owners since 1992. As for eBay and Google, these are still their early days, and they are appropriately reinvesting all their profits. But keep in mind that when you buy a tech stock (or one from any other sector) that doesn't have a dividend, you are speculating that someone will buy it from you for more. In the meantime, you get nothing! You may choose, as I did earlier, to view Google (or the others) as very well-concealed dividend stocks, but you would find yourself in a small minority among your fellow investors, and you would most definitely be challenged by some very difficult present-value calculations.

Before getting back to dividends, let me end this section with another performance observation vis-à-vis buying growth. Which of the following two stock indices has done better: the NASDAQ Composite Index of rapidly growing, tech-oriented companies since its inception in 1971 through mid-2010 or the S&P 500 Utilities Index of mature, high-yielding, profit-distributing utilities? The utility index, *of course*, by 50 basis points per year.[7] For such a long period of time, that's a large gap and a stock market example of the tortoise once again handily beating the hare. Unless you have the time and resources (and sheer luck) to find the one growth stock in a thousand that actually survives, prospers, and begins distributing its profits to company owners, you're simply better off going with the cash returns and the steady if unexciting growth of higher-yielding, higher-payout companies. You may choose to trust in Google, but you should insist that just about everyone else pay cash.

Dividend Growth Only?

If profit growth reflected in dividend growth is the driver of capital appreciation (and together with the base yield, the driver of total return), why not line up behind low-yielding companies that manage to grow their dividends steadily at a high level? My favorite example is Colgate-Palmolive.

While Intel and Microsoft are from the "new economy" where investors are openly indifferent to dividends, Colgate is a storied "old economy" company that manages to increase its distributable profits year in and year out. Though it reinvests most of those profits, the reinvestments generally pay off so there are more profits to distribute each year. Having paid a dividend regularly since 1895, Colgate has a clear commitment to distributing excess profits to the company's owners. It has raised its dividend by 9.1% per year for 48 years (as far back as I have data on Colgate), and over that same period, the share price has risen by 9.6% annually. That is yet another reminder that dividend growth drives capital appreciation. (The difference between the two rates is again explained by the dividend yield being higher at the start of the measurement period than at the end.) The only problem with Colgate, and it's a high-class problem to have, is that buyers and sellers have come to value the company such that its up-front yield is and has been quite low, consistently below 3.0% for the past two decades. That's the rub. Prospective owners are expected to rely on traders and other investors to push up the share price by the 9.0% dividend increase per year. The math still works: a 2.0% starting yield plus steady 9.0% growth in the dividend that comes to be reflected in the stock price still equals an 11% total return. Colgate is a great company, but the issue is how the total return is being generated in any given period: 2.0% in a cash payment and 9.0% in stock movement. From the perspective of a dividend-focused portfolio, that's a lot of reliance on the stock price. It depends excessively on other buyers and sellers recognizing the value of the dividend increases over time. Clearly they have, as the stock price has kept up with dividend growth and then some, but in any given point in time, the cash component of Colgate's return is on the low side.

Consider the Colgate-like scenario from a cash perspective. Take a company with a 2.0% yield and 8.0% long-term dividend growth and compare it with a security that balances a 5.0% current payment and 5.0% dividend growth. Then put $10,000 into both options. In the first year, the low-yielding security will send you four checks worth a total of $200. The other security spins off $500. Just at a basic capital level, you would need another $15,000 worth of the first stock to generate the same amount of cash that the higher-yielding investment does. But the real difference comes in the out years. From a growth rate of 8.0% versus 5.0%, it will take 33 years—yes, 33 years—for the payment from the high-dividend grower to exceed the payment from the high-yielding, slower-growing investment. That's a long time. The higher growth rate looks great, but in the end, it is cash that matters. To quote John Burr Williams yet again, "In short, a stock is worth *only what you can get out of it.*"[8] And through the near-focused lens of Wall Street, even dividend growth itself can be distorted. In 2009 Pfizer cut its quarterly dividend in half from $0.32 to $0.16. And before the little old ladies in Dubuque, Iowa, had a chance to figure out how to make do on 50% less income, the Wall Street brokerages, knowing that we prize dividend growth, began calling us and suggesting, without any sense of shame, that Pfizer would make a good addition to our dividend portfolios because it is likely to start raising the distribution in the next few years. Growing at 8.0% per year, it will take Pfizer nine years just to get its payment back to the previous level. That type of smoke-and-mirrors "growth" holds little attraction for us.

Fixed Income

If the coupon is so important and stocks are so troubling, why not just go all the way to a bond? Good riddance to stocks, and the uncertainty and guesswork associated with them, the argument might go. The coupon of a bond represents a promise to pay, not a choice, as it is in regard to the dividend on the equity, and it is higher up the capital structure in case the company gets in trouble. For clients with a near-term horizon—just a few years ahead of buying a new house, paying a college tuition bill, or even for someone with only a short time to live—I couldn't agree more. Bonds are the right way to go. They offer income, the principal is generally secure, and you can sleep at night. The downside is that, by definition, the coupon is fixed. Over time, the same amount of invested capital cannot produce a rising stream of income. (There are some exceptions, such as inflation-protected Treasuries, known as TIPS.) With life-expectancies lengthening, the baby boomers heading into retirement, and government policies leading to either outright inflation or at least a secular weakening of the dollar, having access to a rising income stream is vital. The trade-off is clear: in return for going down the capital structure from debt to equity and enduring the often volatile stock market, investors leverage themselves to rising income streams.

The attraction of fixed-income instruments can be deceptively high, in part because the fixed-income world is coming off a remarkable 25-year bull run that some investors might extrapolate into the future. In the early 1980s, interest rates were in the teens, and they've been coming down steadily since. That means that fixed-income holders starting in that period collected their coupons *and* saw a significant rise in the value of their principal as interest rates declined. Indeed, in the past decade, most fixed-income investments—Treasuries, investment-grade corporates, high-yield bonds, and municipal bonds—have materially outperformed the stock market, which has struggled to move sideways.

Bonds beating stocks represents a reversal of popular expectations built up during the 1980s and 1990s when investors came to believe that stocks could only go up and would beat the alternatives handily in any measurement period. This view was popularized by Jeremy Siegel with his *Stocks for the Long Run*. Siegel's book was first published in 1994, in the midst of the great bull run of stocks. Even after a decade of poor stock market returns from 2000 to 2009, Siegel's book is still right. In the long run, stocks (as vehicles for current and future dividend payments) offer superior returns, but too many people chose to conclude that stocks would continue to outperform each and every year. Man makes plans; God laughs. Many of the old axioms are true. Having a portion of your portfolio in high-quality corporate bonds is one of them. Here too, the art should be similar to that of dividend investing in equities. What is the ability of management to pay the coupon? If you can't answer that question—I'm channeling Ben Graham here—you are back in the realm of speculation. For diligent bond investors, this type of analysis is normal. That's why, as we look out over the equity universe, we sometimes find ourselves turning to bond analysts for their insights. Good stock work focuses on the coupon, which is what bond investors do for a living. This is another example of what I mean when asserting that the key to successful stock investing is to remove the stock from the equation.

There are many ways to slice the stock market pie: price momentum, positive earnings revisions, low share price, relative outperformance, relative underperformance, small cap, large cap, new economy, old economy, and so on. (As I came up the analyst ranks, I confess I dabbled in some of these styles.) Whether subsets of value or growth, these approaches may "work" for a day, a week, a year, or even several, but none are anchored firmly in a system of cash payments, and all of them require timing a transaction for their alleged superiority to be realized. In contrast, a dividend-focused portfolio delivers a high share of its total return as a cash payment, which is not subject to timing or value determination. The capital appreciation component is also a reflection of something real: the growth of cash distributions in the form of dividends, not the timing of purchases and sales. While there may be many uncertainties associated with investors projecting and achieving that dividend growth, the process at least does not require second-guessing tens of thousands of other stock market participants each and every day as to what some stock might be "worth" a day, a month, or a year hence.

Cash Now!

You should invest in dividends to generate superior long-term total return. That much is clear. But there is another, rather obvious reason to look toward a high-yielding equity portfolio right now: that is current income. Interest rates in this country are at exceptionally low levels, around 3.0% for the U.S. government's 10-year Treasury bill. Near-term interest rates are hovering around 0.0%. If you are lucky, your money market account pays you a penny per month. The yields for the other usual sources of income from financial instruments have dropped in line with Treasuries. The stock market sticks stubbornly to a 2.0% or lower yield where it's been for more than a decade. While a ready supply of income has become scarce, demand is increasing. The baby boomers are now retiring in ever increasing numbers and are looking toward their retirement savings (if they have them) to generate the income needed to pay their monthly bills. A high-yielding portfolio creates the means to do so without having a transaction, without having to engage Wall Street.

Rather than viewing owning a stock as "being in the market," think of it as the way that the monthly electricity bill gets paid. The companies send you the dividend checks; they get passed on to the utility company, to the dry cleaners, to the grocery store. The amount of capital needed to keep the lights on if you are just getting the market's 2.0% yield is more than twice as high than if that capital is generating a dividend yield of 5.0%. Do the math. If your monthly bills as a retiree come to $2,000 per month, you would need a stock market portfolio of $1,200,000 to generate that much income. (This assumes no fees and no taxes, but I'm just trying to make a point.) With the rates on blue-chip bonds as low as they are, you would still need quite a fixed-income portfolio to pay the bills out of interest rather than slowly eating into the principal. In contrast, were the money investing in a dividend-focused stock portfolio with a 5.0% yield, the same $2,000 per month could be met with assets worth $480,000 (again, no fees and taxes). Then there are health care costs. Estimates vary wildly, but seniors having to pay $500–$1,000 per month toward their health care is far from inconceivable. If that is the case, how are they going to meet that need when regular income has all but disappeared from money market funds, CDs, short-term government securities, and high-quality corporate bonds? Retirees may not be accustomed to deriving income from equities, but unless they have a fully funded retirement account, they had better get used to the notion.

3

How Did We Get into This Mess?

The Emergence of Trader Nation

By now, you may well be exasperated and want to know how and when the stock market got so far off the investment track and started looking more and more like a bazaar. This was not an abrupt shift in how the world worked. It occurred gradually over several decades. The retreat began in the early to mid-1980s and gathered momentum during the 1990s (see Figure 3.1). As mentioned earlier, dividend payouts fell steadily from 50% to 30% of net income for U.S. corporations during that time, and many newly listed corporations chose not to pay a dividend at all.

How times had changed. At midcentury, Benjamin Graham had written that a two-thirds payout ratio for mature industrials was about right. (Utilities would have a higher payout.)[1] By the mid-1990s, having such a payout was not a sign of prosperity and stability but of imminent demise. Market observers claimed that companies introducing a dividend or increasing their payouts had run out of growth opportunities. The stocks of such unfortunates might drop 5.0% as the crowd moved on to the next big thing.

The low-payout-is-better mind-set has become so prevalent that one of the leading current benchmarks for dividend

FIGURE 3.1   S&P 500 Index Dividend Payout Ratio (1982 through 2009)

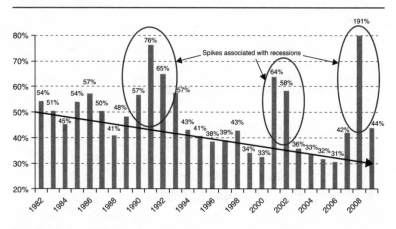

Data from Robert Shiller database, Yale University, http://www.econ.yale.edu/~shiller/data.htm.

investing excludes—yes, excludes—companies with payouts greater than 60%. It's a dividend index that doesn't want dividends; doesn't want those long-term cash-generative and cash-distributive tobacco companies; doesn't want the largest dividend payers in aggregate dollar terms, the phone companies; and doesn't want most of the traditional dividend-paying universe of regulated distribution utilities. While investors are correct to be concerned about companies that cannot sustain their high payout levels—that's what analysts and fund managers are for—the expectations of the investment community in regard to dividends are now just too low.

As you can see in Figure 3.2, as payouts fell during the 1980s and 1990s; the market's yield retreated to its current level of 2.0% or lower from a more normal 4.0% or so.

There have been other periods of low yield and speculative stock excess, but this 25-year run is notably long and

FIGURE 3.2   S&P 500 Index Dividend Yield (1982 to 2009)

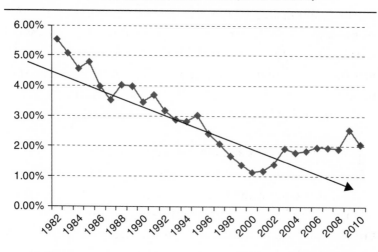

Data from Robert Shiller database, Yale University, http://www.econ.yale.edu/~shiller/
data.htm.

severe. Despite the destruction of stock market capital twice
in the past decade—first the tech bubble and then the general
financial crisis of 2008—investors still think of stocks first
and dividends second. As Graham noted more than a half-
century ago, "A prime characteristic of speculative mania is
its complete insulation from all the lessons of history, whether
remote or directly at hand."[2] Or to paraphrase Hegel, we
learn from history that we do not learn from history. Indeed,
most market participants through middle age have not experienced any paradigm other than "buy low, sell high, repeat
frequently." Yet, if it's so obvious that holding stocks for the
dividend is the key to successful long-term stock investment,
why did we move away from it? How did we become a nation
of traders rather than investors? How did we let the means
become the end and then allow it to stay that way?

The causes are many and overlapping, and the situation is further complicated by the emergence of a discrete bubble in technology stocks in the 1990s. What led to one contributed to the other. Though the tech bubble burst a decade ago, the attributes of Trader Nation have proven more enduring. Let me discuss several of what I believe to be the primary causes of the general public's shift from investing to trading.

Falling Interest Rates and the Perception of Risk

The first and most important cause to me is the 25-year period of declining interest rates commonly associated with former Federal Reserve chairman Alan Greenspan. That sustained reduction of rates to perhaps unnecessarily low levels appeared to cause or at least move in parallel with a decline in perceived risk in all stocks. The so-called equity risk premium tumbled both in the financial math—as it is derived in part from the rates on long-term government securities—and more important, in popular psychology as the perceived riskiness of owning stocks fell sharply.

To some extent, the resetting of the equity risk premium had started more than two decades earlier. In 1958, for the first time, the dividend yield of the stock market fell below that of 10-year Treasuries. Before that time, investors believed that the "promise to pay" of Treasury obligations was more attractive than the "we might pay" proposition of equity dividends. To offset the higher risk associated with holding stocks, they had to have higher cash yields than Treasuries, despite the fact that the stock's coupon could grow over time and the cash return of Treasuries was fixed.

Coming out of the nineteenth century and then the Great Depression, that approach was logical. Stock ownership entailed a (much) higher measure of risk. After the war, with the United States enjoying prosperity and investors envisioning steady growth as far as the eye could see, the thinking about the markets changed. Investors grew comfortable with a lower cash rate of return on equities, offset by higher-dividend growth prospects. Later, in the 1980s and 1990s, with interest rates coming down steadily from the inflation of the 1970s, the NASDAQ or over-the-counter (OTC) market took off and investors came to accept more and more non-dividend-paying equities. Total return from these stocks would come entirely from capital appreciation: buy low, sell high, repeat frequently. It was a 50-year period of economic expansion, rising living standards, and growing asset values across the board. Grandma holding bonds and utility stocks was no longer prudent, it was plain wrong. Internet and technology stocks flooded the market in the 1990s and could only go up. Stocks could "retrace" sharp gains or "consolidate" after a big rally, but as a general rule they could not go down—or so the thinking went.

In the meantime, the perceived value and risk of Treasury investments responded to the same factors affecting equities. In an environment of more or less consistent economic expansion, the "promise to pay" of Treasuries seemed less important than the risk of those flat coupons losing their value to inflation over time. That fear was realized in the 1970s and early 1980s when investors pushed Treasury prices down and yields up to double-digit levels. The market's dividend yield rose as well, though not as sharply, because the main offset to inflation from equities was the ability of corporations to pass through much if not all of the impact in the form of higher dividends.

In late 2008, the markets seemed to reflect, at least briefly, a reversal in investor thinking. The flight to safety pushed Treasury yields down to multidecade lows. Inflation receded as a concern, at least in the near-term, as the 25-year period of credit expansion came to a rapid halt. On the equity side of the equation, yields rose sharply as the market fell, despite dividends being stripped from the all-important financial sector. The lines crossed briefly in December 2008. The implication is the opposite of what it had been 50 years earlier. As the banks have shown in dramatic fashion, a dividend is not a promise to pay, and even institutions with decades-long records of increasing cash distributions can and did find themselves sharply cutting or eliminating their dividends. That risk and the possibility of muted economic growth over the next five years led investors to expect a higher current return from equities than from government securities, which again benefited from their perceived safety. This condition lasted only a few weeks, and the stock market's rapid recovery in 2009 pushed its dividend yield once again below 2.0%, while 10-year Treasury yields moved above the market's cash return. Are we back to "all conditions go"? You can be the judge of that. If we as dividend investors err, we err on the side of caution in that we continue to demand from our equity investments a significant portion of our total return in cash.

In parallel with the decline in interest rates, debt levels in this country took off. As individuals and as a society, we became highly leveraged. The savings rates plummeted to zero and then to a negative level. Total debt as percent of gross domestic product (GDP) shot up to more than 370%. More and more goods and services were purchased on credit. More and more businesses were profitable only because they could borrow capital very cheaply. More and more investments were made with borrowed money. Remember investing on margin to trade tech stocks? Everyone was doing it. The mortgage industry played its role, coming up with products that allowed individuals to use the equity of their homes—

and then some—as a low-cost source of funds to finance life-styles beyond their means.

Major socioeconomic phenomena rarely happen in isolation. Trader Nation emerged against the backdrop of a heightened belief in free markets. Ronald Reagan was elected president in 1980, one year after Margaret Thatcher became prime minister in England. China's process of commercialization was launched under Deng Xiaoping at the same time. The collapse of the Soviet bloc 10 years later seemed to validate the view that free markets were economically superior. That they might be morally superior as well got a lift when Alan Greenspan, an Ayn Rand acolyte, kept pushing for greater deregulation of the financial markets and maintained a dovish (read "low") view of the proper level of interest rates. Others can chime in here with their notions of Kondratieff waves and other long-cycle, socioeconomic analyses. Suffice it here for me to note that free markets do not equate with periods of speculative excess, and unfree markets have their own even worse forms of distortion, led by corruption. But it should not have come as a surprise that a prolonged period of cheap money and financial deregulation would lead to speculative behavior, assuming that other factors permitted or even encouraged movement in that direction—and they did.

Efficient Market Hypothesis

One of the most important other factors behind the development of Trader Nation was the emergence of a "just about anything goes" intellectual framework known as the efficient-market hypothesis (EMH) that gave many market participants theoretical comfort that stocks might actually be worth the sky-high, commonsense-defying prices they were fetching during the various bubbles that investors endured over the past few decades. According to the EMH, as it evolved and spread through academic circles in the postwar period, market prices took into account all available information and that tens of thousands of market participants were rational in their calculations and behavior. "Wrong" prices would be quickly attacked by arbitrage investors who would push prices to their "right" level. What earlier would have been called speculation by Keynes, by Graham, and by just about any dispassionate observer was now considered "efficient." Capital was being allocated to where it would generate the greatest return. The return prospect was supposed to be adjusted for risk, but most investors, particularly individuals, simply left that bit aside. If stocks no longer traded around their dividend yield, there must be a good reason. If money flowed from a company trading at 10 times earnings and with a dividend yield of 4.0% to a company with $5 million in revenue, $50 million in losses, and a market capitalization of $5 billion, that was OK because it reflected the judgment of thousands of investors coming to a rational conclusion based on all available information—or so they said.

A leading proponent of the hypothesis argued that "our postulate thus rules out, among other things, the possibility of speculative 'bubbles' wherein an individually rational investor buys a security he knows to be overpriced (i.e., too expensive in relation to its expected long-run return to be attractive as a permanent addition to his portfolio) in the expectation that he can resell it at a still more inflated price before the bubble bursts."[3] Yet, as recently as 2000, thousands upon thousands of investors were doing precisely that. The EMH is precisely that: an assertion about how the world works. But in its application and popularization, it created vast unintended consequences. As the theoretical physicists tell us, one cannot observe a situation without changing it.

The EMH did so in a bad way, justifying and encouraging all sorts of irrational acts all in the name of rational behavior. It looks self-evidently silly now, but at the time it was considered self-evidently appropriate. I am reminded of the old Soviet anecdote that the daily newspaper *Pravda* ("truth" in Russian) always printed the truth. It's just that the truth could change day to day. That sums up the daily "truth" in the equity markets explained by the EMH.

An early manifestation of the EMH explicitly helped push dividends into the background. It came in the form of an argument by Franco Modigliani and Merton Miller (commonly referred to as M&M) made in 1961 that dividends didn't matter, because investors would be indifferent to total return generated through a dividend payment or a capital gain resulting from a trade.[4] Total return is total return. In flawless math, the authors argued that a higher payout now equals lower dividend growth in the future and the same present value. Simple and elegant: dividend policy is irrelevant.

This is another article that is frequently cited but rarely read. Like Graham and Dodd's work, the 1960s article by M&M is worth tracking down in your local library and reviewing closely. It evokes the now bygone era of moon-shot confidence and absolute certainty buttressed by advances in the social sciences. In this imagined world, "All traders have equal and costless access to information about the ruling price and about all other relevant characteristics of shares. . . . No brokerage fees, transfer taxes or other transaction costs are incurred when securities are bought, sold or issued, and there are no tax differentials either between distributed or undistributed profits or between dividends and capital gains." M&M's world of "'perfect certainty' implies complete assurance on the part of every investor as to the future investment program and the future profits of every corporation." In this environment, dividend policy doesn't matter. Even when M&M allow for an element of "uncertainty" in their world, it is mathematically whisked away as insignificant. Well, that's useful to know. You be the judge as to how helpful equations governing that type of world apply to our all too messy one. Back in the real world of liquidity constraints, transaction costs, differential taxes on capital gains and dividend income, reinvestment risk, and most important, the full panoply of human emotion and behavior, dividend policy does matter.

This is not to say that markets can never be efficient. In fact, the opposite is true. In the long run, markets have to be efficient. Money-losing businesses eventually go away, and their place in the commonwealth and in investment portfolios is taken by profit-making businesses. It is in the markets as it is in society: bad ideas will eventually fail. But in shorter time frames—up to years and even perhaps decades—securities can be regularly and grossly mispriced vis-à-vis their long-term (dividend) prospects. Here again Keynes's oft-quoted comment from the 1930s is apropos: "The market can stay irrational longer than you can stay solvent."

Other Contributing Factors

Tax policy, the deregulation of brokerage services, innovative pension products, and technology also contributed to the move away from long-term investment concentrated on dividends toward a short-term trading mind-set. Changes to the tax code in the late 1970s and early 1980s served the purpose of lowering capital gains rates such that they were well below the rates on regular income, the category into which dividend income generally fell. This situation lasted until 2003, when dividend and capital gains rates were equalized at 15%. The earlier differential rate in taxation encouraged investors to favor capital gains over the steady receipt of income from their equity investments. This structure compounded the consequences of the long-standing double taxation of dividends: they are first taxed as profits at the corporate level and then again as income at the shareholder level. With lower taxes on capital gains, corporate managers could conclude that it was in the best interest of shareholders for companies to buy back their shares rather than pay or increase the dividend. From a shareholder perspective, it appeared to make more sense to buy equities just for capital gains, especially if the gains could be deferred to later tax periods, rather than invest in dividend-paying securities, which created a taxable event (except in retirement accounts) each and every quarter. The large institutional investment managers that emerged in this period may also have played a role in pushing down payout rates as they were generally inclined to play the capital gains game.

Deregulation of brokerage fees in the 1970s provided additional oxygen for the fires of speculation to burn brighter. In the 1930s Keynes had suggested a transfer tax on equity transactions as a way of curbing stock mania. In the 1990s and perhaps even still now, that notion would be viewed as ridiculous. But there can be no doubt that 75 years after Keynes's acute analysis of the Roaring Twenties, the lowering of brokerage fees clearly contributed to the emergence of Trader Nation.

The move from the defined benefit pension plans of an industrial America to the defined contribution plans, IRAs, and 401(k)s of a service America led to more and more stock activity and turnover, although much of it occurred through the intermediary of mutual funds.

And by technology, I simply mean the emergence of the Internet and the World Wide Web that allowed retail investors to go deep and move fast through the market. The intersection of advanced technology and cheap money also created a new category of institutional investor—the hedge fund— many of which adopted near-term, debt-financed trading strategies. All of these factors and others pushed trading into the foreground and investing into the background.

Trader Nation

Add it all up and the result was that average holding periods for U.S. stocks fell steadily to levels not seen since the last great stock bubble in the 1920s (see Figure 3.3). We had arrived at Trader Nation.

Changes should be made in a portfolio (or any business) when they are necessary—to address specific problems—but we shouldn't embrace change for change's sake. Yet all too often the financial service industry encourages turnover that can often seem, and actually is, little more than commission- and paperwork-generating churn. Clients want to believe that they are in control of their financial future, and they are will-

FIGURE 3.3   Average NYSE Holding Period (Years)

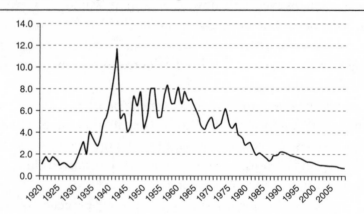

Source: Société Générale, Cross Asset Research, 2010.

ing to pay generous fees to financial advisors to give them that comfort, even if it is an illusion. The pressure on the advisor to trade can be high even when the right thing in the long term might be to do nothing. Similarly, and it bears repeating, most investors never get the nominal returns offered by the markets or even individual financial products, because they can't resist the temptation to *do something*. They end up buying when they should be selling, selling when they should be buying, or as is most likely, doing either when they should be doing nothing at all. We see this type of behavior by investors frequently in our own dividend-focused products. After a short period of relative outperformance, sales take off. And when hot stocks are in and our dividend approach is out of favor, we see redemptions.

Would-be near-term speculators should be doing the exact opposite: buying stocks or mutual funds when they are out of favor and selling when they are at the top of the lists. If they could time that successfully, they would do very well indeed. But it's extremely difficult to time the stock market consistently. So don't try. The better course of action is to put together a dividend portfolio, monitor it for the safety and trajectory of the dividends, make changes when absolutely necessary, and otherwise do as little as possible. As dividend managers, we are often challenged to justify our fees, given that our turnover is so low compared to most other equity products. Our answer is that our work is no less intense than that of other equity managers, but part of the fee is to withstand all the noise, all the phone calls from Wall Street suggesting a great "trade," and to stick to our cash-investing principles when the entire industry is structured to have us do otherwise. In some instances, we earn our manager's fee for steadfastly doing nothing, when we feel that is in the best long-term interests of our clients. (Chapter 4 offers an example of the "Wall Street trade" versus the "dividend-investor hold.")

On the positive side of the ledger, the rise of Trader Nation coincided with a quarter-century of prosperity from the early 1980s through 2007, broken only by two brief and relatively mild recessions. Asset values—the stock market—rose steadily. There's no arguing with success. As the 7 years of fat stretched into 20, the prospect of lean years appeared to recede. Why not participate in those initial public offerings (IPOs) of small tech companies with insignificant revenues and no profits? They only go up, right? Why not start trading stocks for some near-term profits? Everyone else is doing it. The expectation of a cash payment in return for one's ownership stake faded into the background. Investors lost sight of what's important and real, and instead grabbed at the void. A good friend of mine in New York who works in private equity, a line of business quite sensitive to cash-in and cash-out calculations, told me in all seriousness in 2009 that public companies cut their dividends because their stock prices went down. He had become so used to seeing the tail wag the dog that he just assumed it was the natural order.

Returning Cash to Shareholders

During the 1980s and 1990s, the notion that investors would and should be indifferent to dividends worked its way up the capital ladder and began to influence what corporations did with their excess profits. As interest rates fell and investors became less demanding about dividends, corporate managers coming of age in this period became less inclined to pay them. Why should they when the return on the risk-free alternative was declining steadily? A smaller dividend payment and yield would still hold some relative attraction. Also, there were better things to do with the cash. One was to buy growth through wave after wave of merger and acquisition (M&A) activity, most of it value destructive to shareholders but exceptionally profitable to the investment bankers whispering "buy, buy, buy" in the ears of current and would-be corporate titans wanting to hear exactly that. Corporate managers were not entirely responsible for this misuse of excess capital. Boards must also bear some responsibility, approving senior executive compensation plans that encouraged executives to focus on all manner of outcome other than dividend payments to company owners, all in the name, ironically, of "maximizing shareholder value."

Perhaps the most insidious use of cash in lieu of a dividend has been the emergence of the share repurchase program as the preferred means of disposing of unreinvested profits. Why pay or increase dividends when you can buy back shares in the hope of pushing up your share price? With debt being inexpensive, borrowing money to buy in shares could even boost earnings per share (EPS). Without an actual increase in profit from operations, investors might see an increase in their paper wealth. The bias in favor of share repurchases has become so engrained that many companies combine share repurchases and dividends paid together as "cash returned to shareholders." Utter rubbish.

A dividend is a commitment to a direct cash payment to an owner of the company. A share repurchase program is nothing of the sort. It is not a commitment and can be turned off at will. Many are announced with great fanfare; a lesser number are actually executed fully. Their timing is abysmal: as of early 2010, many, if not most, share repurchase programs announced within the past decade were underwater. That is, the shares were repurchased at a higher price than the current one. These programs are typically announced when companies are flush with cash and the stock prices are high. Stock issuances—for instance the banks in 2008 and 2009—are done when the prices are low and the companies need to raise capital. That is, they issue shares at the worst possible moment when capital is most expensive and most dilutive to existing shareholders.

Share repurchase plans also encourage people to go away—to sell their stakes—rather than remain long-term shareholders and collect cash dividend payments. In their worst form, share repurchase programs are designed to simply offset lavish stock-option grants to senior executives. As the options vest and the shares are sold, companies buy them back to keep the overall share count stable. Because many senior executives are compensated on EPS growth, share repurchases, especially with cheap debt, became another way to reward executives, not shareholders, by artificially inflating earnings. It bears noting that share repurchase programs have no cash benefit for existing company owners.

But the greatest hubris behind share repurchase plans is simply that they have the company playing the stock market, trying to buy low and perhaps sell high, when it should simply be running its businesses. The recent decision by Deutsche Telekom to lower its dividend to fund a share repurchase program is an example of this type of thought. What does a widget maker (phone company) know about the stock market? Perhaps the chief executive officer (CEO) of a brokerage firm could claim that he or she ought to be encouraged to buy back shares opportunistically because it is a core competence, but for the other 99.9% of public companies, they have little excuse other than that they have been encouraged to do so by Wall Street itself, which benefits directly from the turnover.

Paying cash to company owners through a dividend generates no trading revenue. There is no M&A associated with it, no advisory services, no underwriting. Obviously, brokerages and investment banks have little interest in recommending that companies simply pay and increase their dividends. As an institutional investor, I often have cause to visit company executives in their own offices. If I see a Bloomberg terminal, a very expensive market monitoring tool, in the chief financial officer's (CFO's) or worse yet in the CEO's office, I have to ask myself are they spending too much time trying to manage their stock—time that should be spent managing their businesses?

The announcement of a share repurchase program or "insider" buying by a senior executive has come to be viewed by market observers and the financial media as a signal that a stock necessarily represents great value and must be going up. While it is true that company executives have asymmetric information about the condition of their businesses, they generally know no more about the stock market than anyone else. The value of their company is set every day at 4:00 P.M. through negotiations involving thousands of buyers and sellers who may or may not have a view as to the near-term or long-term value of a business. (Mutual fund managers selling to meet redemptions are not making long-term calls in the same way that putting new funds to work does not necessarily represent a change of view about investments that are held.) Company managers have little control over the process. Whether they successfully purchase their company's stock will have more to do with the general trend of the market—if it's going up, as it did in the 1980s and 1990s, share repurchases look good, as does insider buying —than with the value of the declaration to purchase shares.

In recent years, I can think of only one instance when I was persuaded that a share repurchase program was the right thing to do. It was during the market dislocation of 2008 and 2009 when a rural phone company was trading with a midteens yield. The market was pricing in a dividend cut, but our analysis showed that the company's cash flows easily supported the dividend. In that case, the company's use of its excess cash to repurchase shares served to very efficiently reduce dividend "leakage" and helped protect the admittedly high dividend that our clients were receiving. At the time, we encouraged the company to consider a special dividend that would confound the casino traders who assumed the dividend would be cut. That was a little too radical for the management team, and they opted instead for share repurchases to take advantage of the period of extreme valuation. The market and the company's stock soon recovered, and the yield returned to its more typical high single-digit level.

If you will indulge one last observation about the extent to which companies allowed the stock market to drive their business thinking, I must mention those firms that have integrated it directly into how they compensate their executives. Over the past several decades, total shareholder return (TSR) schemes in which relative or absolute stock price performance figured into compensation packages became popular. They amounted to letting the fox into the henhouse. If you are a businessperson, imagine that rather than being compensated for increasing sales, upping profits, improving returns on capital and so forth, you are instead compensated on whether someone in New York; Greenwich, Connecticut; or London has put in a higher or lower bid on your business that day, regardless of their knowledge of what you do or their long-term interest in investing in your company. That doesn't make much sense, but it happens all the time.

One positive consequence of a decade of sideways movement in the stock market is that TSR schemes are less the rage than they once were. When we consider companies for investment, we check to see whether and to what extent stock price performance on an absolute or relative basis plays a role in incentive compensation. While we might choose to own a company that does, we clearly prefer those that pay their senior executives on the basis of internal operating metrics over which they can have at least some control. If they are effective in increasing those metrics, we are confident that the value of the business (as well as the cash distributions we receive) will rise.

The Industry of Trader Nation

The brokerage industry is as old as the stock market, but in the past 25 years, the infrastructure in support of Trader Nation has grown vast. Legions of people now make a living creating and then trying to take advantage of near-term stock price movements. Corporate managements participate in the process through endless investor presentations at which the company provides "guidance" for earnings per share that it then beats by a penny or more—funny that. In many instances, the company has provided that guidance just a few weeks or so before the end of the quarter, when it presumably had pretty good visibility to its operations. Then it beats, and Wall Street celebrates. A naive observer might conclude that the company was intentionally misleading investors when it issued its guidance or that its forecasting skills, even for near-in events, are pretty poor. In either instance, I have to wonder whether we as dividend investors want to be a minority owner of a company led by that type of management team. Unfortunately, if we excluded every large corporation that ever "played the game," we wouldn't have much to choose from, but we remain strongly averse to such practices.

Brokerages

As troubling as the behavior of many corporations has become in recent decades, it is the brokerages that get top billing on the Trader Nation marquee. If you are not aware of how brokerages make money, you may be excused for not seeing them as part of the problem. As their names suggest, brokerages facilitate trades between buyers and sellers and keep a small bit for themselves. They also trade the firm's own assets. News that leads to trades and price swings is good for business—the more trades the better for them. A long-term investment strategy such as dividend investing isn't really subject to near-term news and doesn't lead to a lot of trading. So rather than encourage investors to clip coupons four times a year, the brokerages issue reports every day, telling investors to buy or sell a certain security. A few months later, they'll issue another report recommending that investors reverse the trade. Whether or not investors profit from this advice is hard to say, but the brokerages most certainly do. I am still amazed to see lengthy, detailed research reports on companies with 5.0% or 6.0% dividend yields from leading brokerages—where the "really smart" analysts are employed—that make no or little mention of the dividend, even when at those yields, the components of total return are likely skewed very much toward it. These reports may contain valuable information that really does shed light on the company's dividend prospects, but you wouldn't know it from a superficial reading. The authors of these reports see only stocks and trades. That's how they get paid. In contrast, the brokerages don't make a penny when a company pays a dividend. It doesn't get a commission when a company chooses to increase its dividend rather than repurchase shares via the brokerage. It earns no advising fee when a company chooses to distribute its profits to its owners rather than go out and buy another company. Ever wonder why dividend investing doesn't get a lot of attention? Because there is no money in it for Wall Street.

As the manager of a dividend-oriented strategy, I often ask myself why brokerages even bother competing for the modest trading commissions our business generates by providing us with research. If the broker does offer good information about a company's business trends that helps us conclude not to trade—because we're already holding a security with a positive dividend outlook or because we're not holding one that has poor prospects—we have no way of paying for that service. It's silly, but it is how business is done on Wall Street. They should charge cash. Fortunately, more and more investment firms are moving to fees paid by individual investors based on assets under management rather than transactions. That's a huge step in the right direction. The research-for-trading commissions model at the institutional asset management level, however, is still awaiting a long-term solution.

The Equity Style Box

Beyond the brokerages, the financial services industry offers a wide array of products and services in support of Trader Nation. Financial advisors, consultants, and managers exist to make profits for the vendors of those goods and services. Fewer than we would like to imagine do so by actually generating superior returns for their clients. No single product captures that phenomenon as well as the equity style box. You have probably encountered this with your advisor—a nine-box matrix that divides the stock world into the subjective categories of growth, core, and value, and then subdivides them again into large-cap, mid-cap, and small-cap. Much of the investment advisory world makes a living by regularly altering the allocations among the various boxes and rotating managers within each box who outperform, on a relative basis, the other managers in the same box. The goal of near-term relative outperformance of another manager in the same style has taken over, while meeting actual client needs for income and total return has receded. Finding and tracking a good "mid-cap value manager" may or may not help you pay for a child's college education or prepare for retirement, but it definitely keeps a small army of advisors, consultants, and managers employed.

The standard equity style box as it has emerged in Trader Nation paradoxically does not even have a square for the approach that offers superior long-term total results: one focused on dividends. Given that there exists a vast industry that is supposed to help investors maximize their returns from the stock market, this seems rather odd. It's not surprising that many of our advisor clients struggle in this environment to determine where to place our dividend-anchored portfolio. From my perspective it is a "core" strategy, reflecting how the market once was and how it will likely be again. Some accept that; others find room for it as a boutique, almost exotic, allocation that gets squirreled away in a particular style box, usually on the "value" side. On one hand, it is folly not to have a place in an allocation framework for capturing the dominant role that dividends play in total return. On the other hand, to simply create a sub-box for dividend stocks while retaining the basic box structure only prolongs the existence of a framework that does not serve investor interests. As with stock prices, investors have let the means become the end. Advisors are trained to fill all the boxes, not to meet real customer needs. The financial services industry does very well out of that process; the client is fortunate if he or she does as well.

Over the next decade or so, I wouldn't be surprised to see the style box evolve drastically so that it is better aligned with real investor needs (e.g., income) than the version that emerged in the 1980s and 1990s in an ever-rising market. After a decade of flat returns, the shortcomings of the style box are becoming evident. Proponents of the current system will argue the opposite, that in a market moving sideways, the nine-box system offers investors the means of accessing products that are working well now, and it can help them move on to the next big thing when it occurs. Trader Nation triumphs again. If those transitions can be consistently well timed, then they should be pursued by risk-taking traders. But the likelihood of the retail investor finding the secret formula to frequent trading is as low today as it was a decade ago, fifty years ago, or a century ago.

Benchmarks

Benchmarks are much the same as style boxes. In Trader Nation, investment managers are measured against benchmarks, which are supposed to capture how they perform vis-à-vis their opportunity set. In theory, it sounds quite reasonable, but in practice, the benchmarks are just a further manifestation of the style box phenomenon. They do not measure the ability of managers to make money for clients; they measure the relative performance of managers in a particular style box. Relative performance is all that matters. Up until the early 1980s, I would have considered the S&P 500 Index to be an appropriate benchmark for a dividend strategy. It was a core strategy; that was the core benchmark. In the age of Trader Nation, however, with the S&P 500 Index consistently yielding less than 2.0%, the broad market benchmark cannot be used as the direct, near-term measure of performance of dividend stocks or dividend managers. Longer-term, of course, the broader market's low yield works to the advantage of a dividend manager. Simple mean reversion—the observation that most things in nature and society revert back to long-term trends—all but guarantees that a high-quality, dividend-oriented portfolio will beat the S&P 500 Index when the latter has a starting point of a 2.0% or lower yield, as it does now. Recall that higher yield beats lower yield over time, and 2.0% is a very low yield.

Consensus Earnings Estimates

Consensus earnings estimates also rank high on the list of perverse practices in Trader Nation. When you hear that a company beat the "consensus" for the quarter, you have to appreciate the highly stylized theater that is being put on for your benefit. The brokerage analysts have their quarterly earnings estimates. These are gathered and in some cases scrubbed—outliers removed—by a third party and disseminated through the financial media as the consensus number. This fictional number then takes on a life of its own. It is discretely managed down by the company in question so that it can "beat" expectations by at least one penny per share. In stock market psychology, simply meeting expectations represents a failure; beating becomes critical. The history of those expectations are kept and chronicled so that traders have the opportunity to identify companies with positive earnings expectation revisions. Computer models will then take into account the history of earnings beats and revisions to earnings expectations. The result is that something that is completely made up, an expectation of near-term and generally meaningless EPS, becomes a determinant of real value, at least for a day or a month. Quarterly earnings and the quarterly consensus estimates tell you essentially nothing about a company's dividend trajectory over the next three to five years or longer, which is what you as a company owner should care about.

Corporate Near-Termism

The impact of the market's near-termism is not limited to individual and even institutional investors. It influences companies, which, though they deny it strongly, clearly feel compelled to "make the quarter" and manage their businesses accordingly. If you as a small businessman have a rough month or two, do you quickly sell a building or part of your business or time a tax event just so you can show a near-term profit that someone might have been expecting for you, even if you knew that such a step was not in your long-term interest? Of course not, but when all eyes are on the stock market, where publicly traded businesses "reprice" daily and U.S. companies have to bare all on a quarterly basis, that is precisely what happens. I mentioned earlier that most large, mature, dividend-paying companies are publicly traded and are therefore subject to these near-term pressures. But not all. Mars (packaged confection), Cargill (food ingredients), and SAS Institute (business intelligence/data analysis) are among the largest U.S. corporations that you may have never heard of. They are mature, and they very likely pay handsome dividends to their owners. But as the shares are not traded on a public exchange, they are not subject to the same scrutiny as their publicly traded peers. That condition allows their managers to make decisions (or at least try) that are in the best long-term interests of the shareholders. Unfortunately we can't tap into the cash streams of successful private companies, as much as we might like to. The paradoxical offset of allowing investors to get into and out of a stock on a daily basis is that the very same ability may actually undermine the point of the investment: tapping into high and rising dividend streams. The means get in the way of the end. Except for that small subset of investors who have ready access to dividend-paying, dividend-growing private companies and can let the capital sit there for a long time, going through the stock market ranks as a necessary evil for the modern dividend investor.

What's the Problem?

At this point, you may be asking: what's the point? The world is the way it is, validated each and every day by people who accept it. They function within its existing practices and boundaries that evolve in a direction most individuals consider an improvement over time. Is it not the height of arrogance to claim that the market is "wrong" in how it has come to operate over the past quarter century? Every day thousands of market participants negotiate the price of securities. More buyers than sellers, and the price goes up. More sellers than buyers, and the screen shows red. What's wrong with that? And if the market is so wrong, why do so many people put so much money into it? For taxable savings, there are many alternatives. And even in tax-deferred accounts, there are other asset classes (although not so many) where investors could avoid equities.

On a basic level, there is nothing immoral, unethical, or (generally) illegal about inhabiting Trader Nation. The challenge for most investors is to generate the long-term return (or better) that equities purport to offer. The chief risk they face is that they ignore the components of total return—dominated by dividends—in favor of trading strategies and overpaying for growth stocks. For retail investors in particular, Trader Nation is a bit like Las Vegas. It looks easy and you may get lucky now and again, but the odds are very much in favor of the house, and the longer you play by the house rules—trading rather than investing—the less likely you are to have a positive experience. And then there are the professional card players.

As I write in 2010, Goldman Sachs's proprietary trading desk has been crowned the most recent king of short-term trading for its ability to have profitably navigated the financial crisis of 2008 and 2009. Various hedge funds have held that title for years at a time over the past two decades, back to the very smart people at Long-Term Capital Management in the 1990s who supposedly brought a renewed mathematical rigor to trading. It worked until it didn't work, which wasn't too long. That's the problem with Trader Nation, even for the pros. Few asset managers can materially beat the market for more than a brief period of time through short-term strategies. Most (but not all) of those strategies take advantage of momentum, which ultimately reverses, and few managers time that reversal correctly. So the impressive near-term gains are given back. Mean reversion may be the most powerful and obvious force in nature, but timing it is an entirely different issue. All the while, the short holding periods typical of Trader Nation leave dividends playing a role that is incidental at best. Unsupported by cash returns, traders are entirely reliant on finding individuals to buy the stocks (corn futures, baseball cards, condos in Florida) for more than they paid for them. That potentially high-return and certainly high-risk way of making a living should be antithetical to long-term, mainstream investing. Trader Nation is fine for those who love taking risk, who crave daily swings in their portfolios, who dream of making it big by finding the next Google before everyone else does. For the rest of us, it is a place characterized by lots of turnover, high fees, subpar returns, and complicated taxes.

The implications for society are even broader. The capital markets—debt, private equity, public equity—serve to allocate resources and are a central means by which free societies grow and prosper. Turn that capital allocation process into a big betting parlor and the country will eventually suffer. I can do no better than to quote Keynes again: "Speculators may do no harm as bubbles on a steady stream of enterprise. But the position is serious when enterprise becomes the bubble on a whirlpool of speculation. When the capital development of a country becomes a by-product of the activities of a casino, the job is likely to be ill-done."[5] What is at stake is not just the private matter of small-town retail investors or even the fortunes of hedge fund managers. What is at stake is the future of our nation. Human nature being what it is, speculation and the temptation to indulge in it will always be with us. The issue is one of balance. After a 25-year binge, it is time to shift back to a more balanced investment culture, where speculation is limited to its proper realm: high-risk and or highly cyclical ventures known to be such and priced accordingly.

After two market crashes in the past decade and the damage wrought by the EMH, we are likely at a turning point. I say "likely" because the sustained decline in interest rates that has contributed so much to the emergence of Trader Nation is over. Rates are close to zero for near-term fixed income instruments. On a nominal basis, they cannot go lower. In extreme times like these, it is natural to look back in history to see what, if anything, can be learned from similar episodes of speculative excess. The most relevant one appears to be the period leading up to the Great Crash of 1929. During the Roaring Twenties, speculation was also at the forefront of investor activity. After the Great Crash, a series of thoughtful observers—Graham and Dodd (1934), Keynes (1936), and Williams (1938), among others—diagnosed what had happened and recommended how stock investment ought to be pursued. Seventy-five years is a long time. Veterans of the 1920s and 1930s are gone. Individual memories are short; institutional ones are even shorter. And in no case do they extend three-quarters of a century back.

For our generation of financial service professionals, the Great Crash and the risk of repeating it are ever so remote. While the specific causes of the 1920s bubble and the more recent period of speculation are different, the outcomes were nevertheless quite similar: a wide range of overvalued securities owned by a risk-taking and leveraged shareholder base. So if I refer back to these authors from the 1930s so often, it is because they try to answer many of the questions that are now being asked about our markets. Chapter 12 of Keynes's *General Theory* should be required reading for anyone opening a brokerage account, as should the original Graham and Dodd, not the Warren Buffett gloss on it. But my personal favorite is the underappreciated work of John Burr Williams, *The Theory of Investment Value.* Though it should be widely read today, his 600-page, equation-filled tome is unlikely to change popular thinking about the markets. But besides the added historical perspective and going light on the math, I am telling investors little beyond what Williams wrote in the late 1930s.

4

How to Invest for Dividends

Do It Yourself—or Not?

So now that you've seen the logic of using the stock market as a means of tapping into distributed cash flows and have come to at least a basic understanding of how and why investors got away from deploying their capital in that manner, the question becomes what do you do next? On the one hand, the news is good: investing prudently in a high-yielding, dividend-growing strategy in a market with such a low yield all but guarantees long-term outperformance of that market, with low turnover and a straightforward, easy-to-understand approach. On the other hand, investing in this manner in what is still a relatively hostile environment—that same low yield, low payout, and generalized indifference to dividends— is quite challenging.

Your first task is to determine whether to do it yourself or pay a professional. That is, do you conduct the company research yourself, and pick and maintain a dividend-focused portfolio for that portion of your financial assets that you wish to invest in this style? A lot of the basic research can be done over the Internet from the comfort of your own home. For brokerage services, E-Trade, Schwab, and Fidelity will be happy to accommodate you at minimal cost. Or do you turn to a financial advisor to put you into products (mutual funds, separately managed accounts [SMAs], individual securities, etc.) that focus on dividends? Only partly out of self-interest do I strongly, earnestly recommend the latter course of action. The fact of the matter is that there is a great deal of work required to make sure that the theory, history, and math outlined in this book actually perform as expected in your account. As full-time managers of dividend-focused products, we have substantial human resources and technology at our disposal. As a typical individual investor with a day job, do you have the means to investigate thoroughly and track the companies in which you've become an owner? To paraphrase Ben Franklin, a person who casually manages his money by himself has a fool for a financial advisor.

It's not that using a financial advisor guarantees you will make a lot of money, but due to the risk controls and systems that most retail brokerages and financial advisory networks have put in place in the past few years, it should lower the chance that you will lose a lot of money. After a decade of lousy stock returns and stomach-churning drama in the equity markets, brokerages and advisory networks are shifting away from products designed to make a "quick buck" (but too often ended up losing it) to products and systems that are designed to protect and preserve client capital. That being said, the financial services industry is still part of the problem (recall the dangerous place called Trader Nation) and there are still many financial advisors who could themselves use a tutorial in dividend investing. So the following section aims to prepare you to have an intelligent discussion with your broker or financial planner. If you insist on going out and purchasing individual securities, this section reviews some of the tools that we use in the everyday management of our dividend portfolios. It is a summary, not a full accounting, but should give you a sense of what it is to assess stocks based on their dividend prospects.

Balancing Dividend Yield and Dividend Growth: The 5 + 5 Portfolio

Of the two elements of the strategy—dividend yield and dividend growth—the former is pretty easy to spot. Almost all the basic investment websites and data sources carry the annual dividend and the yield (the dividend divided by the current price). It follows that coming up with a high-yield portfolio is a not a difficult task. The real challenge, and where the portfolio manager earns his or her fee, is in making sure that the dividend is safe and that the dividends can grow. Those are the two components of total return, and they must both be present. But where is the balancing point between dividend yield and dividend growth?

That's a fair question, and the answer is that it depends. As much as the dividend investor seeks distance from the daily hurly-burly of the stock market, it constitutes our opportunity set, and its daily price-setting mechanism determines the initial yield of our portfolio for prospective clients. (The realized yield for any given client depends on the yield at the time of purchase and any subsequent dividend changes, not on the daily closing price of the stocks.) With the S&P 500 Index yielding less than 2.0% (roughly the same level for the past decade) and with dividends removed from the financial sector, high-quality, secure coupons at the lower end of the yield range have become more attractive. Nevertheless, investors still need to insist that the total return pattern be clearly skewed toward the dividend. If you've reviewed the present value section in Chapter 1, you know why. If you skipped over it, suffice it to say that the higher the (secure) yield, the quicker you are getting your money back from your investment. As a practical matter, that means securities should generally have a yield of at least 3.0% and preferably even more than 4.0%, materially higher than the market's low cash return of 2.0% and the equally uninspiring, roughly 3.0% coupon of the so-called risk-free alternative, 10-year U.S. Treasury bills.

The actual security selection process starts not with the easy-to-see yield, but with analysis of the company's dividend growth prospects. The foundation question at the center of our process concerns "the ability and inclination of management to pay and increase the dividend by an appropriate amount over the next three to five years." That time frame is short by dividend standards but absolutely epochal for most investors nowadays. For companies at the high-growth end of the spectrum, with realistic dividend trajectories of 6.0% –8.0% or so, we can tolerate a lower (but not too low!) upfront yield of perhaps 3.0%–4.0%. Many high-quality, consumer and consumer-oriented health care businesses fall into that category.

At the other end of the spectrum are mature enterprises, such as the phone companies, with more limited dividend growth prospects. That's fine too. They need to reinvest less of their cash profits and can distribute most of them to the owners of the company. As a result, the yields can be very attractive: 6.0%–8.0%. Even if they grow revenues just in line with gross domestic product (GDP) and raise their dividends 2.0%–4.0% per year over a five-year period, they can still play a role in a portfolio. Combine the two elements, along with those in the middle that have a more balanced return pattern (roughly 5.0% yield, 5.0% dividend growth), and you have a high-yielding, dividend-growing portfolio where the long-term total return is entirely captured by and driven by dividend payments and growth in dividends. (And the stock market, we rejoice, has been essentially squeezed out of the equation.) But you need both. A security with an attractive yield—say 5.0% or 6.0%—but no prospect of dividend growth in the foreseeable future doesn't work for us. As you recall from Chapter 1, that looks like a bond and limits the opportunity for an increase in the value of the investment. That is, the stock is not likely to go up. At the other end of the spectrum, relying primarily on dividend growth in the future while only getting a minimal yield at present leaves the investor too dependent on the company actually achieving those growth expectations and on the stock market recognizing them.

Having the total return of the portfolio come from the combination of dividend yield and dividend growth is a simple restatement of the Finance 101 formula for the value of an investment known as the Gordon Constant Growth Model[1] where dividend growth has replaced the variable for earnings growth that can no longer be trusted due to Wall Street shenanigans. We often simplify it further by referring to it as the 5 + 5 portfolio: 5.0% yield plus 5.0% dividend growth. That's in line with the historical 10% return of the market (really between 9% and 10%, depending on the starting year), but it's actually a conservative estimate of the prospective long-term total returns from a dividend-focused strategy, as the dividend segment of the market has historically done quite a bit better than the market's customary "10". As a practical matter, there are clear benefits to investing in this pattern (5 + 5) of cash distributions as opposed to relying primarily on the stock market and trading to generate total return.

First, about half of the annual return over longer measurement periods comes from the ongoing, regular cash payment we can feel very confident we will receive. No transaction or buyer is required. That means the volatility (i.e., the degree to which our total return jumps around in any given measurement period) is much lower than for a strategy where the returns are all stock based. There are various technical ways to measure this, but the evidence is clear: dividend strategies have lower "standard deviations" than non-dividend-focused approaches. Some people—traders, brokers, and hedge fund managers—love volatility. Up and down creates lots of trades, commissions for brokers, opportunities for a quick profit for the hedge fund community, and mountains of paperwork for accountants at the end of the year. Investors will do just as well without all that excitement.

The second benefit is that the focus on dividends allows investors to disengage from most of the news, activity, and noise on Wall Street. Yes, the balance of supply and demand every day between 9:30 A.M. and 4:00 P.M. sets the price of securities, which in turn determines the dividend yield of any given stock. (It changes every day, although the dividends do not.) But that's where the dividend investor's engagement should end. Once we have come to our conclusion about a company's dividend growth prospects and decided that the current yield is attractive (or not) in light of those prospects, there's not much point in having a lot to do with the stock market–focused media. So much of the information content— essentially all of it—coming from Wall Street is near-term in nature and stock price in focus. Very little of it is relevant to the long-term trajectory of profit growth and even less in regard to the distribution of those profits. Think of all the "news" provided by the brokerages and the financial media circus: quarterly earnings previews, broker rating upgrades and downgrades, and slight revisions of earnings expectations for a single quarter. Then there are the famous or rightly infamous penny "beats" and "misses" of broker "consensus estimates," which are largely the result of guidance from the companies themselves. This is the stuff that occupies people who trade stocks for a living. Good luck to them. It is extremely hard to master for long periods of time.

By focusing on the much smaller determinants of long-term value—the dividend and dividend growth as reflections of underlying profitability and long-term profit growth—dividend investors do well not so much by what they do as by what they choose *not* to do. Pick your fights carefully. Benjamin Graham's advice many decades ago couldn't be any truer now: except for times of extreme valuation (very low to buy; very high to sell), the true investor "will do better if he forgets about the stock market and pays attention to his dividend returns and to the operating results of his companies."[2]

In short, turn off the tube. Here the purported statements about Warren Buffett, whether true or not, are spot-on for the dividend investor. He is supposed to have answered a question as to when he makes money by answering, "when I sleep." And the man is said to use the computer on his desk simply to play bridge, his well-known hobby. (Other sources suggest no computer at all.) The point is clear: Warren Buffett doesn't spend his time staring at stock prices and putting trades through. Again, the key to successful stock market investment is to take the stock out of the equation; it is just a means to an end. As for the over-the-top vendors of stock information that you see on television—the media pundits, and sellers of day-trading software that promises triple-digit returns—you have to ask: if they have such a good bead on the market, why aren't they managing money directly rather than telling others how to do so?[3]

Buy, Hold, Sell

The 5 + 5 algorithm sounds straightforward enough, but how do we actually execute it in the portfolios? Or, as we are often asked, what is our "buy," "hold," and "sell" discipline? These are stock market terms, but as we collect our rising coupons from publicly traded companies, the question is reasonable. And you should not be surprised to learn that all three processes are the same and are derived directly from the dividend. This is to say, they are a step or two, or more, removed from the stock market.

Stocks are purchased as described earlier: working backward from the dividend growth and determining what is an appropriate initial yield. From that point on, the hold discipline doesn't really involve the stock market. As long as a company continues to pay and increase its dividend in line with our expectations, we have little reason to consider changing the position. Again it is helpful here to take the stock out of the equation and to think of the portfolio as a business, one that as long as it is making regular, large, and modestly growing cash distributions to us as owners of the enterprise does not need to be disrupted just because the "bid" price someone might offer us for the business is less (or more) than it might have been yesterday or the day before. There is no need to resort to Wall Street's commission-generating "target" prices, sector "rotations," conviction "buys" and "sells," benchmark underweights or overweights, or the other tricks of the financial industry trade. Why should we? As long as the dividend streams coming into the portfolio continue to rise, the value of those businesses will follow suit. In an ideal situation, we have no need to trade at all. We collect the coupons, and the stocks move up as the dividends do.

The sell discipline is similarly dividend related, but in one of the two scenarios, the stock market does play a role. That scenario is when the share price outstrips dividend growth. The best recent example was in the middle of the last decade when real estate investment trust (REIT) stocks became very popular. Although the dividends continued to rise in line with profit growth, investors bid the stocks up and the yields down to intolerable levels. REITs are pass-through securities designed to distribute (or pass through) essentially all of their profits to shareholders. As pass-throughs, they do not pay tax at the corporate level, which leaves more cash to be distributed to company owners. As generally slow-growing distribution vehicles, REITs traditionally have had high single-digit dividend yields. But in 2006, many of them were considered growth stocks and saw their yields fall below 5.0%. For the dividend investor, a REIT with a yield less than 5.0% and a low single-digit dividend growth rate doesn't make much sense. If I sound apologetic for having to sell a security because it went up too much, I almost am—but only almost. REITs are good diversifiers, are associated with the real economy, and historically have had a record of being low-volatility investments. Selling them because they had gone up too much meant facing reinvestment risk—finding a place to put the proceeds that would achieve similar goals for us. In the end, taking advantage of the market's inefficiency—REITs soon fell back to earth—made sense. Being on the right side of a small speculative bubble ended up being profitable for dividend investors, but it was not the point. Over the long term, it would be better to do without all the excitement and trading and just collect a stream of rising coupons.

The second form of sell discipline represents a less happy outcome. We can and occasionally will get the dividend question wrong. That is, we might have concluded that the company can pay and increase its dividend for the foreseeable future, but either be wrong in the initial assessment or have the business environment change so drastically that individual companies will be forced to cut their dividends. We may spot the mistake or the change in the business conditions early enough to get out having preserved most of the invested capital. It can then be redeployed to safer income streams. In other instances, such as the financial crisis of 2008, the problems can mount so quickly that by the time an investor concludes that the dividend is at risk, the reduction of the capital base has already occurred. Those events aren't common, but when they do occur, the damage can be tremendous.

It is because bad things do on occasion happen that you will want to have your stock portfolio diversified across numerous securities and economic sectors. The academics disagree over how many separate stocks are required to secure the benefits of "diversification," but most professionally managed equity portfolios have at least 30 or so individual securities in them. If you are doing this on your own, you will also want to tap into various dividend streams to lower the risk of being exposed to a single company or, as in the case of the financials in 2008, an entire sector where the dividends come under siege.

In other instances, large, mature companies that are generally dividend friendly can shift course and decide to spend billions in acquisitions in the hope that they can either buy growth or the illusion of growth through cost cutting at the combined entity. Most acquisitions fail to live up to expectations; almost all large ones do. In recent years, Pfizer cut its dividend to buy Wyeth, and Kraft passed on dividend growth to buy Cadbury. They changed course and as a result, so did we. If a slow-growing large company tells you that it's going to buy another large company so that it can improve its growth profile, be wary, very wary. Shareholders likely won't fare well from those deals, but remember who most certainly will: the investment bankers who collected hundreds of millions of dollars in cash for "advising" both parties. They have no vested interest in what happens to existing shareholders who were collecting the dividends. They've already moved on to the next big deal.

What Do We Look For? Cash, of Course

So having identified a return profile that we like (5 + 5) and having screened the stock market for the type of securities that we are looking for (yield greater than, say, 3.0%; market cap above a certain basic threshold; and a history of dividend growth), how do we then answer our foundation question regarding "the ability and inclination of management to pay and increase the dividend over the next three to five years?" The question is simple to pose, but far more difficult to answer. The process involves two forms of analysis: business and financial.

Business comes first and feeds into the financial framework, but as a practical matter, we actually work backward and look first at the company's financial statements. If you run your own business, you'll already be familiar with the three main ones: the income statement, the balance sheet, and the statement of cash flows. If not, it would help to dust off your Accounting 101 textbook and review it. (If you don't have the time or the desire to review the basics of accounting, then this would be yet another reason to use a professional money manager. It's what they do for a living so you don't have to.) So that you can follow along with a real-world example, I've also included the financial statements (see Tables 4.1 to 4.3 that follow) from Kimberly-Clark Corporation's 2009 annual filing on Form 10-K with the Securities and Exchange Commission (SEC). I've not included the company's quarterly releases or its quarterly filings. Except in those instances when something extreme has happened in a firm's business during the course of the year—and those events tend not to be in dividend companies to begin with—you are better off focusing on the annual filings. Leave the quarterly filings, the monthly brokerage reports, and the daily swings in the stock prices to the speculators.

Free Cash Flow (FCF)

At the end of the day, a dividend payment is cash—not earnings, not company guidance, not Wall Street's consensus "number," not long-term stated goals in a PowerPoint presentation, but cold hard cash, coin of the realm. It's what you use to pay your bills; it's what you should expect from your investments. So to consider how safe the dividend might be and whether it might reasonably grow, we work backward from the last of the financial reporting forms: the statement of cash flows. Once there, we start with the company's free cash flow (FCF): the money from which the dividend will be paid and the object of our analytical focus. (Wall Street will sometimes have you look at earnings before interest, taxes, depreciation, and amortization [EBITDA] as another definition of cash flow. It is not useful in regard to dividend analysis, which has to be paid out of funds remaining after interest, taxes, and capital expenditures, just like the payments your business might have to make.) FCF is usually not calculated in the reporting form, so you may have to do the math yourself. But it is quite simple: cash flow from operations minus capital expenditures. Is the resulting FCF figure rising or falling? Is it steady or highly variable year to year? Does the FCF equal or exceed—"cover"—the dividend payment (farther down the statement of cash flows), and has the coverage ratio deteriorated or improved in recent years?

TABLE 4.1   Kimberly-Clark Corporation and Subsidiaries Consolidated Cash Flow Statement

	Year ended December 31		
	2009	**2008**	**2007**
	(millions of dollars)		
Operating Activities			
Net income	$1,994	$1,829	$1,951
Extraordinary loss, net of income taxes, attributable to Kimberly-Clark Corporation	—	8	—
Depreciation and amortization	783	775	807
Stock-based compensation	86	47	63
Deferred income taxes	141	151	(103)
Net losses on asset dispositions	36	51	30
Equity companies' earnings in excess of dividends paid	(53)	(34)	(40)
Decrease (increase) in operating working capital	1,105	(335)	(330)
Postretirement benefits	(609)	(38)	14
Other	(2)	62	37
Cash provided by operations	3,481	2,516	2,429
Investing Activities			
Capital spending	(848)	(906)	(989)
Acquisitions of businesses, net of cash acquired	(458)	(98)	(16)
Investments in marketable securities	—	(9)	(13)
Proceeds from sales of investments	40	48	59
Net (increase) decrease in time deposits	(47)	76	(10)
Proceeds from dispositions of property	25	28	97
Other	—	14	(26)
Cash used for investing	(1,288)	(847)	(898)

continued

TABLE 4.1   Kimberly-Clark Corporation and Subsidiaries Consolidated Cash Flow Statement, *continued*

| | Year ended December 31 | | |
| | 2009 | 2008 | 2007 |
	(millions of dollars)		
Financing Activities			
Cash dividends paid	(986)	(950)	(933)
Net (decrease) increase in short-term debt	(312)	(436)	43
Proceeds from issuance of long-term debt	2	551	2128
Repayments of long-term debt	(278)	(274)	(339)
Cash paid on redeemable preferred securities of subsidiary	(53)	(47)	
Proceeds from preferred securities of subsidiary	—	—	172
Proceeds from exercise of stock options	165	113	349
Acquisitions of common stock for the treasury	(7)	(653)	(2,813)
Shares purchased from noncontrolling interests	(293)	—	—
Other	(26)	(51)	(34)
Cash used for financing	(1,788)	(1,747)	(1,427)
Effect of exchange rate changes on cash and cash equivalents	29	(31)	8
Increase (decrease) in cash and cash equivalents	434	(109)	112
Cash and cash equivalents, beginning of year	364	473	361
Cash and cash equivalents, end of year	$798	$364	$473

As you can see in Table 4.1, Kimberly's cash from operations has been on the rise in recent years, from $2.4 billion in 2007 to $3.5 billion in 2009. That's rather more than slow, steady growth, but at least it's heading in the right direction. After taking into account capital expenditures, FCF has grown from $1.44 billion to $2.6 billion. Kimberly's steadily rising dividend payment, still less than $1.0 billion in 2009, is easily covered by its FCF. If the FCF is less than that of the dividend being paid out, you should understand that the company has been drawing down cash reserves or borrowing money to pay the dividend. It's also helpful to compare the FCF per share to earnings per share (EPS). In a mature business, the two figures should be quite similar. If they are not, we want to make sure we understand why. A large discrepancy between the two can be a sign of opportunity or heightened risk to the dividend. But to understand which, we need to delve into the source of the discrepancy.

Capital Expenditures

To analyze the trajectory and components of FCF, we need to move up (and in some cases off) the financial statements and work our way backward to the first line of the income statement, sales. But there are many stops along the way. The first stop is capital expenditures (CapEx): spending on big-ticket items such as plant, property, and equipment. What is the trend in CapEx? Is it steady or volatile? In many industries, CapEx is measured as a percent of sales. Is that ratio rising or falling? Kimberly's CapEx has actually been declining modestly (see Table 4.1). To see that in a growing business suggests greater productivity of the assets being put to work or the end of a multiyear build-out that involved above-average equipment expenditures. It can also signify that a company is underinvesting in its business. Note that in Kimberly's case, CapEx remains about 10% ahead of the annual depreciation charge for wearing out equipment. That type of ratio seems about right for Kimberly's business profile—mature domestic markets and investment in emerging markets. In short, Kimberly does not appear to be ignoring the needs of its plant, property, and equipment.

In a steady-state business, CapEx and depreciation should be about the same. In a rapidly growing business, CapEx will almost certainly be much greater than depreciation. But even mature, noncyclical industries go through spending cycles when they will have elevated CapEx. For instance, for the past several years, the staid and sober, dividend-safe regulated distribution utilities with straightforward (not too high) dividend payout ratios have been spending vast sums on infrastructure investments. The combination of their capital expenditures and their dividends exceed their FCF, by quite a bit. Ordinarily that could be a sign that the dividend needs to be cut, but that outcome is unlikely in the case of the regulated utilities. They have easy access to the capital markets and can raise the difference from investors. Better yet, they can rely on an essentially guaranteed return on the capital raised because of the regulated nature of their operations. That is, the fact that the utilities are FCF negative for a few years while they invest in the nation's electric infrastructure doesn't necessarily mean that they can't pay and increase their dividends. Still, if given a choice, we want even our utilities to generate more FCF than they pay out in dividends. If they are going through a big CapEx cycle, we need to spend extra time and effort to make sure that they are not taking on too much debt, that they can get the return that they are expecting, and therefore that we can reasonably expect the FCF to once again start covering the dividend.

At the other end of the CapEx spectrum are companies that for whatever reason have minimal capital expenditure requirements. Two industries come to mind. One is tobacco. As we observed earlier, cigarette consumption in this country is declining rapidly. Manufacturers are consolidating their operations and merging into one another. As a result, CapEx levels are low, often well below the depreciation charges of the existing plant, property, and equipment. For these companies,

FCF may be more than net income and can support a dividend payout at or even above EPS. A similar example comes in an unexpected quarter: the telecommunications industry. Much like the cigarette companies, the rural landline phone companies (rural local exchange carriers, RLECs) operate in a declining business environment as more and more individuals shift to cell phone only and turn off their old Bell landline. And like the cigarette companies, the RLECs have business models based on consolidating a declining industry and managing costs closely. For these companies, FCF is often well above net income due to minimal capital expenditures versus still substantial depreciation charges. The result is that the companies can support very high dividend payouts. Without further consolidation, this model can't go on very long and does require close monitoring, but it does explain why the dividend investor is so focused on CapEx and its impact on FCF.

Pension and Retiree Benefit Costs, Working Capital, Cash Taxes, and Depreciation

The next stop on the statement of cash flows is the accounting nightmare known as pension and retiree benefit costs. (This line item can have various names. For Kimberly, it is called postretirement benefits in Table 4.1.) Fewer and fewer large U.S. corporations still offer defined benefit (DB) pension plans, having shifted new employees to defined contribution (DC) programs such as 401(k)s. But these DB programs are still on the books for many mature U.S. companies, and shareholders are on the hook to make them good. The accounting for these programs is horrific. Suffice it here to say that if the bean counters feel that a company's program lacks sufficient assets to cover the plan's future obligations, cash contributions from the company will be moved into their plan, which can be seen in the pension and retiree benefit cost section of the statement of cash flows. That's what happened in 2009 at Kimberly, when the company made an additional cash contribution to its pension plan.

There's a great deal more to postretirement obligation analysis, but we spend quite a bit of time trying to understand the impact of a company's underfunded pension plan (very few of them are overfunded) on dividend and dividend growth. At the extreme end of the risk scale, pension obligations and postretirement medical benefits played a big role in undermining not just the dividends at the U.S. auto manufacturers but also the companies themselves. At a minimum, we want to make sure that we feel comfortable about the "funded status" of the pension plans of the companies that we invest in. Much of the information that we use to make that determination is located in the notes that accompany the financial statements in the annual report. If you are passionate about discount rates and actuarial assumptions, you will really enjoy doing this part of your due diligence. If not, you have yet another incentive to employ a professional.

Working capital is another big contributor to the difference between net income and FCF. Fortunately, it's also much more accessible to the investor, especially if that person manages his or her own business and intuitively understands the interaction of inventory, accounts receivable, and accounts payable, and their impact on the cash in the till. Net working capital is roughly the first two (inventory and accounts receivable) minus the third (accounts payable), and for large corporations it is usually expressed in relation to overall sales. Here the questions are similar to those asked about CapEx: what are the ratios, and how have they been changing? Companies rarely get into dividend trouble due to working capital issues, but it can be a harbinger of other troubles if the company's change in working capital line is outsized. Indeed, for mature companies, the absolute number ought to be quite small. In contrast, rapidly growing firms will generally consume cash in the form of working capital as they build out inventories and accounts receivable, only partially offset by trying to string out paying their own vendors, the accounts payable line. By the time a company becomes a big dividend payer, there shouldn't be much activity going on at the working capital line. Kimberly generated cash from working capital in 2009 after two years of seeing it consume modest levels of cash (Table 4.1). According to the discussion in the annual report, reductions in inventories and a rise in accounts payable were the primary reasons behind the improved cash performance.

Not surprisingly, almost no large U.S. corporations pay in cash the nominal tax rate on profits that they show on the income statement. The difference shows up as the deferred taxes line in this section of the statement of cash flows. Like changes in working capital, it shouldn't be a big issue in the analysis of dividend safety, with one exception. For a variety of reasons, companies may have exceptionally low cash tax rates due to losses in previous years and other tax shields. Should those benefits cease or diminish, the company's actual cash outflow can increase and leave less cash for dividend growth or even payments. If you see a big swing in the deferred tax line, you should investigate further.

Finally, you'll note depreciation (and its sibling amortization). It is subtracted as a charge from the income statement, but because it is a noncash item (mostly for wearing out plant, property, and equipment), it is then added back in on the cash flow statement. It gets analyzed in tandem with the CapEx number. For a mature company, the two figures should be roughly in line with one another. The more the company is growing, the greater the difference one would expect between CapEx and depreciation.

Balance Sheet Review

The top line of the statement of cash flows is the same as the last line of the income statement, net income. But before moving back there, the dividend investor needs to make a stop at the balance sheet (see Table 4.2). This measure of a company's assets and liabilities is synchronic. That is, it is a snapshot in time, usually December 31st or the end of the company's fiscal year. In contrast, the income statement and statement of cash flows are diachronic: they are measures of what has happened over a period of time, a quarter or a full year. The difference is important. For instance, the balance sheet will tell you how much a company owes in debt, but not how much debt has been added or reduced in the past 12 months.

TABLE 4.2   Kimberly-Clark Corporation and Subsidiaries Consolidated Balance Sheet

| | December 31 | |
| | 2009 | 2008 |
	(millions of dollars)	
Assets		
Current assets		
Cash and cash equivalents	$798	$364
Accounts receivable, net	2,566	2,492
Inventories	2,033	2,493
Deferred income taxes	136	131
Time deposits	189	141
Other current assets	142	192
Total current assets	5,864	5,813
Property, plant, and equipment, net	8,033	7,667
Investments in equity companies	355	324
Goodwill	3,275	2,743
Long-term notes receivable	607	603
Other assets	1,075	939
	$19,209	$18,089

Liabilities and stockholders' equity

Current liabilities

Debt payable within one year	$610	$1,083
Trade accounts payable	1,920	1,603
Accrued expenses	2,064	1,723
Accrued income taxes	79	103
Dividends payable	250	240
Total current liabilities	4,923	4,752
Long-term debt	4,792	4,882
Noncurrent employee benefits	1,989	2,593
Long-term income taxes payable	168	189
Deferred income taxes	377	193
Other liabilities	218	187
Redeemable preferred and common securities of subsidiaries	1,052	1,032

Stockholders' equity

Kimberly-Clark Corporation stockholders' equity

Preferred stock—no par value—authorized 20.0 million shares, none issued	—	—
Common stock—$1.25 par value—authorized 1.2 billion shares; issued 478.6 million shares at December 31, 2009, and 2008	598	598
Additional paid-in capital	399	486
Common stock held in treasury, at cost—61.6 millions shares and 65.0 million shares at December 31, 2009, and 2008	(4,087)	(4,285)
Accumulated other comprehensive income (loss)	(1,833)	(2,386)
Retained earnings	10,329	9,465
Total Kimberly-Clark Corporation stockholders' equity	5,406	3,878
Noncontrolling interests	284	383
Total stockholders' equity	5,690	4,261
	$19,209	$18,089

Debt is visible on the balance sheet; the repayment schedule is in the notes accompanying the balance sheet. Determining how easily a company can service its debt involves these figures as well as the funds (from the income statement) available for ongoing interest obligations or the repayment of principal. These are fairly straightforward ratios. The harder task can be to determine and analyze off–balance sheet liabilities. They may be disclosed in the footnotes; they may not be. If the business model or the company's history makes us wonder about off–balance sheet liabilities, we investigate. Finally, while the cash component of meeting postretirement or pension obligations is reflected on the statement of cash flows, the truly arcane accounting for these liabilities is presented in its full glory on the balance sheet and in the accompanying notes. For fear of losing you after promising a light read, I'm simply going to mention that it exists and that it can affect the cash available for the payment of the dividend and most certainly the growth in that payment. In sum, Kimberly's balance sheet (Table 4.2) does not raise alarms about the dividend. Nothing stands out. No entries are outsized, nor were there any dramatic changes from the previous year's snapshot.

Above and beyond concerns about debt and retirement obligations, reviewing the balance sheet is critical for analyzing the dividend prospects of banks and most other financial service companies. While most nonfinancials earn and pay their dividends in ways that can be seen on the income statement (and confirmed on the statement of cash flows), the financials are different. As regulated entities, they have to maintain a certain amount of capital, which can come either from investors or from retained profits. Their dividends are then paid out of the capital in excess of what the company must, or chooses to (if it's more), keep on the books. The income statement serves to measure what's happening to that pile of capital—either increasing via profits or decreasing due to losses. So whereas for nonfinancials, the dividend comes out of earnings with a nod to the capital base in case the company runs into near-term trouble, for financials it is the opposite: the dividend is paid out of capital with a nod to whether it is increasing or decreasing due to operations reflected on the income statement. As a practical matter, answering our foundation question for the financials involves reviewing a lot of balance sheet ratios, the performance of loans, and the difference between what banks pay for their capital versus what they realize for loaning out that money.

How's Business? The Income Statement Review

After reviewing the balance sheet, we return to the income statement, and that means we're back to business. The income statement (see Table 4.3) is the representation of how a business is basically doing: products, sales, cost of goods sold, margins, marketing, administrative expenses, profits, and so on. At the end of the day, is the company earning its dividend? What is the payout ratio, the dividend per share divided by the net income per share? (Kimberly's earnings have been rising, albeit unevenly. They are well in excess of the dividend of $2.64.) How have those figures changed in recent years? And what are the trends likely to be in the next few years? We try not to make too many detailed forecasts, as that isn't a very useful exercise. Recall that the dividend isn't anywhere near as volatile as quarterly or even annual earnings, so spending a lot of time on figuring out the next quarter's earnings "number" just doesn't make much sense. And trying to come up with a precise earnings figure for five years out may be a fun academic exercise (if you are so inclined), but the further out we go, the less precise we are likely to be. Instead, we spend a great deal of time examining a company's business outlook, its product cycle, distribution channels, competitors, and so forth.

TABLE 4.3   Kimberly-Clark Corporation and Subsidiaries Consolidated Income Statement

	Year ended December 31		
	2009	2008	2007
	(millions of dollars, except per share amounts)		
Net sales	$19,115	$19,415	$18,266
Cost of products sold	12,695	13,557	12,562
Gross profit	6,420	5,858	5,704
Marketing, research, and general expenses	3,498	3,291	3,106
Other (income) and expense, net	97	20	(18)
Operating profit	2,825	2,547	2,616
Nonoperating expense	—	—	(67)
Interest income	26	46	34
Interest expense	(275)	(304)	(265)
Income before income taxes, equity interests, and extraordinary loss	2,576	2,289	2,318
Provision for income taxes	(746)	(618)	(537)
Income before equity interests and extraordinary loss	1,830	1,671	1,781
Share of net income of equity companies	164	166	170
Income before extraordinary loss	1,994	1,837	1,951
Extraordinary loss, net of income taxes, attributable to Kimberly-Clark Corporation	—	(8)	—
Net Income	1,994	1,829	1,951
Net income attributable to noncontrolling interests	(110)	(139)	(128)
Net income attributable to Kimberly-Clark Corporation	$1,884	$1,690	$1,823
Per share basis			
Basic			
Before extraordinary loss	$4.53	$4.06	$4.11
Extraordinary loss	—	(.02)	—
Net income attributable to Kimberly-Clark Corporation	$4.53	$4.04	$4.11

Diluted

Before extraordinary loss	$4.52	$4.05	$4.08
Extraordinary loss	—	(.02)	—
Net income attributable to Kimberly-Clark Corporation	**$4.52**	**$4.03**	**$4.08**

How distinctive is our analysis of the business? Not very. It's just basic business analysis, and if you want to understand what might allow a company to have and grow its distributable cash in a variety of economic environments, my advice to you is to go to the library and get an older book on business analysis. My preference for the dust-covered texts is simple: the old verities about competition and market share, about product development and marketing, about capital budgeting and working capital management, and about industry cycles still hold true. Yes, it is the case that globalization has changed the market size and the competitive set. It is certainly true that the Internet has advanced marketing, communication, and distribution. Probably the best of the recent innovations is supply chain management, which really has revolutionized manufacturing and distribution businesses and dampened the economic volatility earlier associated with inventories. (The question remains whether the inventory cycle has simply been replaced by other sources of cyclicality.)

The goal, however, is still sustainable sales and profit growth—and that has not changed. Nor have the tools changed dramatically. If you need to know about disruptive technologies, consider the role of the internal combustion engine a century ago. Think business networking via the Internet is new? Attend a Rotary meeting in your local neighborhood. LinkedIn.com may be an improvement on Rotary, in the same way that the Lexus is an improvement on the Model T, but it is not fundamentally different. Business models do evolve, paradigms do shift, but let's not get carried away about how new "new" is.

During the Internet bubble, investors got away from the old business verities in the same way they got away from dividends. They began accepting clicks in lieu of cash. That ended poorly. Note that the most recent wave of new-economy companies, such as Google and many of its peers, have profitability built in from a much earlier stage. These companies may not be relevant (yet) for dividend investors, but they are a great improvement over the profitless business models offered as public equity investments 15 years ago.

Investors and participants in the housing and financial services bubble that burst in 2008 also ignored old truths and common sense. They thought leverage (debt to equity) of 30 times would be fine for investment banks. The same was true of lending money to people who could not possibly afford to pay the loan back and placing them in houses well beyond their means. These "subprime" loans, which were bundled together and then cut into tranches of various "quality" as determined by a rating agency paid by the investment bank putting it all together, was akin to building a house of straw, painting it brownish-red, and selling it as brick construction. The most recent crisis was not complex. Though dressed up in elaborate mathematical models and presented in a bewildering array of product acronyms, it was actually very, very simple: you can't make something from nothing. If you start making a very lot from nothing, as Wall Street did, you should not be surprised when the whole structure comes crashing down.

So if our business analysis boils down to just a calm application of common sense, what is distinctive about the process? As I mentioned earlier, it's not so much what we do, as what we don't do. Unlike the vast majority of our peers, we don't spend time trying to figure out what our investments might be worth to someone else a week, or a year, or five years from now. How many angels can fit on the head of a pin? We don't really care, and neither should you. Dividend investors are in the cash collection business, so you don't need to waste your time with "target prices" or Wall Street's endless commentary about how a stock is "cheap" or "expensive." Instead, focus on what matters: the *amount, quality,* and *trajectory* of a company's cash payments to its owners. The amount should be ample relative to the price paid to make sure that the math of present value works for you, not against you. The quality should be high. It shouldn't be borrowed, based on exceptional profits that could disappear tomorrow, or be the result of a temporarily very low cash tax rate. And finally the trajectory should be positive, likely to grow in line with GDP or somewhat better over the next three to five years for the mature, higher-payout companies, and at a higher rate for those companies still finding good investment opportunities for their reinvested profits. Treat the investment as you would one in a private business—that dry cleaner down the street, the bakery around the corner, or the small apartment building near a college campus. The only difference is this business investment happens to occur through the stock market. But let me repeat once again a central tenet of this book: the key to successful stock investing is to take the stock out of the equation.

Inclination

In most instances, the accounting review just outlined is pretty straightforward. The analysis of business conditions that might support continued payment of a rising dividend is a good deal more difficult because you are forecasting general operating conditions and specific company performance forward, but it can be done, particularly for larger, mature enterprises whose businesses tend to be stable over time. That is, we can feel comfortable having a view on Kimberly-Clark three or five years out. We would not have such confidence forecasting the future of the latest hip retailer (remember Krispy Kreme) or a boom-and-bust materials company. But what about "inclination," the second metric in our foundation question regarding "the ability and inclination of management to pay and increase the dividend over the next three to five years?" How committed is management to paying and growing the dividend? Would they cut it to finance a large acquisition? If they got into a patch of trouble, how quick would they be to lower it? Would they sacrifice the dividend to support the credit rating on their debt? Even for companies where the chance of a cut is remote, we ask ourselves whether management is inclined to limit the growth of the dividend in order to fund a share repurchase program or serial acquisitions. How high does the dividend rank on management's list of priorities?

Answering this part of our foundation question is as much art as science and another reason why it pays to have a professional look into it. Here are a couple of tools that we deploy. The first is history. CEOs of companies with long track records of dividend payment don't want to be the guy on the watch when the dividend gets cut for the first time in a century. That's how they lose their jobs. The Coca-Cola Company of Atlanta, Georgia, has paid a dividend every year since 1920. Procter & Gamble in Cincinnati has paid every year since 1890 and raised its dividend every year since 1956. Those types of companies have shareholders such as pension funds that rely on the dividend and expect the company to pay unless disaster strikes. Having declared a dividend every year since 1903 and increased it annually since 1972, the regional bank BB&T was a dividend stalwart until the financial crisis forced it to cut its distribution in early 2009. It is the exception that proves the rule. History is not a precise road map to the future, but it is a helpful guide. We prefer companies that have paid dividends for a long time, have investors for that very reason, and are managed by individuals who understand that the investors are there in large measure for the dividend.

The dividend history of a company is relatively easy to look up, and we can assume that Coca-Cola's and Procter & Gamble's management understands why investors consider it important. But there are many younger and smaller companies out there without that sense of direction or purpose, and for those, extra analytical effort around the "inclination" of management is required. That is particularly the case after our recent 25-year pendulum swing away from dividends. Many corporate managers who have come of age in this period are surprised by the notion that their primary responsibility to the owners of the company is to make rising cash payments to them. For these cases, we want to speak directly and frankly with management about their intentions. Wall Street offers, in fact sells, access to corporate managers through investor conferences, road shows, and field trips. Some of these can be useful to us as dividend investors to better understand a company's business prospects. But more often than not, these stage-managed gatherings are a waste of time for us.

For instance, at a recent small group meeting with the chief financial officer (CFO) of a major European phone company, my discussion about the dividend outlook was impatiently endured by a hedge-fund investor sitting next to me who, when given the opportunity, interjected, "Enough about the dividend. Let's talk about the stock." He could not have cared less about the dividend; his hedge fund probably wouldn't own the security long enough to collect it. That's typical of the atmosphere of these meetings. They are focused on what's going to affect the share price in the next few months or quarters. The dividend gets scant attention. At the end of the day, the European telecom in question chose to cut the dividend and use its excess cash to repurchase shares. Chalk one up for the hedge funds and Wall Street.

Instead of duking it out with the traders, we prefer to travel to company headquarters and meet management directly, without the "help" of Wall Street brokers. As large institutional investors, we can usually get the access we seek, but it does require a willingness that many small investors and most hedge funds don't have: to leave the confines of New York City; Greenwich, Connecticut; Boston; and London. In contrast, we're happy to travel to Monroe, Louisiana, and Little Rock, Arkansas, to spend time at the headquarters of the leading rural phone companies; to Irving, Texas, to visit the management of Kimberly-Clark; to Raleigh, North Carolina, for Progress Energy; to Indianapolis in the case of Eli Lilly; to San Ramon, California, for Chevron; and to Long Beach, California for HCP (a large health care REIT). Critics charge that this type of research introduces another behavioral bias: getting too close to management and taking what they say at face value when in fact they are painting too rosy a picture or when they themselves have a poor grasp of the future. Both charges can be correct, and information coming from just one session with management, regardless of the location, isn't very useful. That's why we repeatedly meet with the managers of our portfolio companies. That they may intentionally or unintentionally mislead investors is a given, but we focus on how their manner of discussing business conditions or their commitment to the dividend has changed since our last meeting. Has their characterization of the dividend's importance altered? Is the body language of the CEO or CFO in regard to the dividend different from what it had been earlier? For smaller companies in particular, this type of checking in is critical. The trick is not to visit a company once and think you have the inclination part of the equation solved, but to see management regularly to have what we call "the conversation."

The conversation works both ways. In addition to listening for changes in tone and presentation, we also want to communicate to the executives. For those companies getting frequent calls from Wall Street bankers about better things to do with their cash than pay and increase the dividend, we want to make sure that far away from the canyons of New York, we have the opportunity to explain firmly to the company that we hold the stock for the dividend.

We let them know that if they listen to the investment bankers, they will lose us and others like us. The conversation generally goes smoothly with the long-standing dividend payers—utilities, telcos, and many staple companies—but in other instances, there can be a clear divergence of opinion about capital allocation. In those cases, if we don't feel sufficiently convinced about inclination, we'll invest our clients' money elsewhere.

The large pharmaceutical companies are a good example of a sector where some mature, ought-to-be obvious dividend payers fall short on the inclination front. The industry faces clear, specific challenges, but its main obstacle is that it has gone "ex-growth." That is, revenues and profits across the board are no longer consistently growing at double-digit rates. Yet, many managers there still have the growth mentality. They believe that if they throw enough money at a problem, they can fix it. Both Pfizer and Merck have "resolved," or so they would say, their growth issue through large acquisitions.

One cut the dividend to finance the transaction; the other has kept the dividend flat for the better part of a decade. These companies have legitimate challenges, but they are large, mature enterprises with excess profits. It's time for them to wake up and smell the coffee. Our conversations with these executives can be tense. As owners or prospective owners of the company, we're not only listening to them outline their plans but also telling them at the broad-strokes level how they should be allocating capital. Sometimes they break our way, sometimes not. When they don't, it is unfortunate for dividend investors, but even in the dividend-challenged U.S. market, there are plenty of other fish in the investment sea.

5

Putting It All Together

Thinking Long Term

Sounds easy, right? Particularly if you can sidestep some of the tricky pension accounting and don't mind a lot of time on the road visiting companies. But there is a catch, a big one, and it's another reason why you should consider using a professional and, perhaps even more difficult to do, have the courage to turn off the TV and basically ignore the stock market. The problem is that in a market yielding 2.0% and with the financial services industry and most investors defining *long term* as next week and *total return* as how much their stocks have moved, those securities having big yields (higher than, say, 4.0% for anything other than a utility) are seen as having big problems. To have such a high yield, the popular thinking goes, the stocks have either been declining or have stayed flat while the dividend rose over time. The Wall Street analysts will say that something is wrong with these companies: they have no growth opportunities, their industries are declining, or whatever the issue may be. Generally, though, the main thing wrong with these businesses is that they are out of favor with investors who are quite happy to pay 20 times earnings and 50 times (2.0% yield) the cash dividend for a company whose long-term prospects may not be materially better than a company trading at 10 times earnings and 25 times the dividend (4.0% yield). Of course, sometimes the stock market crowd is correct and a high yield really does signal issues that the business is in a rut or, worse yet, that the dividend may not be sustained. That's why we have a staff of analysts monitoring our holdings and any changes in the answer to our foundation question. That's what we do: spend our time among the high yielders figuring out who can and who can't pay going forward. That's why simply buying high-yielding securities and hoping for the best is a poor substitute for an active, ongoing review process.

Telecom Dividends

Telecom stocks over the past few years are an almost perfect example of the opportunity that the stock market's near-term focus inadvertently provides to long-term dividend investors. As of 2010, dividend yields within the space are exceptionally attractive. AT&T (T) and Verizon (VZ) both have yields between 6% and 7%.[1] The rural phone companies, CenturyLink (CTL) and Windstream (WIN), are generating cash returns of 8%–9%. The leading global telecommunication vendors, Vodafone (VOD) and Telefónica (TEF), offer yields in the range of 6.0%–7.0%. The largest Canadian phone company, BCE (BCE), has an annual dividend worth 5.5%–6.0% of its current price. In contrast, the S&P 500 Index has a cash return of less than 2.0%. In as much as the components of long-term total return are dominated by the dividend, particularly the basic yield, the telecom sector's absolute and relative return prospects are quite notable. Though only 3.0% of the S&P 500 Index as currently constituted, the U.S. telcos represent around 9.0% of the total dividend opportunity in the broad market index. (That does not include the large foreign phone companies.) In a sideways-moving market environment in which the dividend yield may well be all that you get for the next few years, the telcos stand out.

The other significant component of total return is dividend growth, and despite the sector's high current yield, which implicitly casts doubt on the security of those payments, the dividends have been on the rise. AT&T and Verizon both raise their dividends annually by an amount (2.0%–4.0%) that is consistent with their high payout and mature growth profile. Despite a "flat dividend" model, CenturyLink recently increased its distribution by 4.0%. Outside the United States, Vodafone has been raising its dividend steadily and is on track to continue doing so for the foreseeable future. Telefónica has explicitly committed to a significant increase of its dividend payout ratio and its actual dividend to 1.75 euro by 2012. Since returning to the public equity markets after a failed leveraged buyout (LBO), BCE has raised its dividend numerous times and has signaled its ability and intention to move toward a higher payout.

Dividend yield is only relevant if the dividend is safe. While the recent and prospective increases discussed earlier speak volumes about the underlying financial condition of the companies making the payments, it is worth reviewing the financial ability of these companies to support their payouts. These companies operate in a mature sector; their reinvestment needs are modest so they can support the 70%–80% payout ratios of AT&T, Verizon, and Telefónica. BCE is lower at 65%, and Vodafone is lower still at 53%. In the case of the landline-only rural local exchange carriers (RLECs) CTL and WIN, with substantial depreciation charges and minimal reinvestment needs, company management can pay out essentially all of the profits. As discussed earlier, the free cash flow (FCF) payout is more useful than the income statement payout alone as this takes into account both capital expenditures and depreciation charges. Here the situation is even more accommodating. The dividends at the majors represent only about 50%–70% of the FCF produced by those companies. That is, they can easily pay their dividends from the cash that they generate. The greatest difference in regard to the earnings payout and the FCF payout can be seen, however, in the RLECs, which have FCF payouts of just 50%–60% compared to the 100% nominal income payout. Follow the cash.

Aren't these companies highly leveraged, and isn't that a risk to their dividends? Yes and no. Cash flow at these companies is quite steady, so they can handle debt more easily than cyclical companies. Verizon, AT&T, Vodafone, and Telefónica are all "A" rated companies. Granted that designation isn't as helpful as it used to be, but these are not companies on shaky ground. BCE is just one notch lower at BBB. CenturyLink comes in at BBB–. Windstream is the only "high yield" name in the bunch with a BB rating. The major incumbents have debt coming due steadily, but will have no difficulty refinancing it. Indeed, one of the benefits of having sustained, artificially low interest rates over the past few years has been that high-quality companies such as the telcos have been able to refinance their debt at attractive rates and reduce their debt service costs. The debt repayment schedule for the rural phone companies is not challenging. Windstream's next large tranche is due in 2013, CenturyLink's in 2016. Further out in the future, the phone companies have substantial pension and retiree health care obligations, but to judge by the price of telco debt, the bond community is not too concerned about the condition of these companies. Verizon's and AT&T's 10-year bonds are trading with a yield 150–200 basis points (1.5%–2.0%) below that of the equity. That's the reverse of the usual situation in the low-yielding U.S. stock market, where most stocks trade with yields lower than that of the bonds from the same company. Not so in regard to the telcos.

If everything for the phone companies appears to be copacetic, why is the market pricing their equity such that the yields are so high? Keep in mind that the stock market isn't very good at focusing on the long term. Human emotion and the overwhelming news flow encountered every day make it hard for individual investors and many pros to make good long-term decisions. The telcos provide an excellent example of this myopia. Skittish investors see competition in the United States—from struggling Sprint Nextel and minor players who operate in the prepaid wireless segment as well as from the cable companies competing in broadband—and regulatory threats in Europe in the form of declining mobile termination rates (MTRs) that are pressuring revenue and profit growth in the industry. These are legitimate concerns. This is a mature industry, and growth is slowing. Customers are dropping their landlines quickly, and most of the adult population here and in Europe already have cell phones and broadband service in one form or another. After years of robust growth, this shift to maturity has some investors spooked.

What they don't see—in addition to the basic dividend yield, which is so crucial to total return—is consolidation. It goes hand in hand with maturity. In Europe, essentially all the data points speak to consolidation, through outright mergers or through cooperative agreements that reduce expenses by getting rid of duplicative infrastructure and administrative costs. In the United States, the process is even clearer. Decades ago, television audiences chuckled at Lily Tomlin on "Rowan and Martin's Laugh-In" on NBC as our none-too-helpful operator for the "the phone company." Now after a drawn-out process of deregulation and fragmentation, we are well on our way back to having "the phone company," dominated by the duopoly of Verizon and AT&T. The remaining contenders, Deutsche Telekom's T-Mobile and especially Sprint Nextel, are struggling to find a strategic niche. The small vendors focus on the prepaid segment at the low end and will eventually be absorbed or consolidate themselves. As the consolidation proceeds, pressure on pricing will abate, and the companies can resume increasing profits in line with gross domestic product (GDP) and perhaps somewhat better due to the scale of their operations. Given their current yields, investors don't need to see earnings growth of more than 2.0%–4.0%, reflected in dividend growth of the same amount, to justify an investment. For the rural phone companies, consolidation is not part of the business plan, it *is* the business plan. Windstream and CenturyLink have emerged as the Verizon and AT&T of the landline industry, consolidating the industry even as it shrinks.

Other near-term knocks on the phone companies may well end up benefiting them. One has been the troubles iPhone users experienced in recent years on AT&T's network, especially in New York and San Francisco. Investors also chose to see the introduction of Skype, the Internet phone service, onto mobile devices as a defeat for the phone companies because it further cuts into their profitable voice business. Both challenges are real, but they are both near term and will likely facilitate the return of usage-based pricing. That is, for the first century or so of phone service, customers paid by the minute, by the amount of service that they consumed. For the last decade or so, all-you-can-eat pricing—a flat monthly rate for essentially unlimited service—has come to the fore. Fortunately for the phone companies, the iPhone and the likes of Skype make flat pricing untenable. I don't expect to see Candice Bergen on TV anytime soon once again offering 10-cent-per-minute long-distance plans for Sprint, but the return of usage-based pricing is inevitable. Instead of being for voice services, however, the usage-based plans will be for data. Stream video all day long on your iPhone, and you can expect to pay more than your office mate who occasionally checks the weather.

Near-term puts and takes aside, on balance the telcos offer an exceptional proposition for investors with long-term horizons and a preference for cash returns. Time will tell, but being the tortoise generally works out very well. It may take years before the business thesis plays out and even longer before it is recognized by the stock market, but dividend investors can just quietly wait, collecting the 6.0%–8.0% coupons from these "troubled" companies, and try not to smirk too much as the dividends rise 2.0%–4.0% per year.

A Tale of Tissue

Let me provide another example of dividend investing in practice, one that highlights the risks of playing by Wall Street's rules. As you should now appreciate, dividend investors tend to be on the dull side. We eschew the excitement of the near term in favor of investments in steady, modestly growing companies that usually aren't all that flashy. Those companies—often providers of everyday necessities—generally have excess profits and can afford to return a good portion of them to shareholders in the form of cash. That may seem a heretical notion on Wall Street, actually sending out a check to the client, but it's what we like to see and we are not going to apologize for it. These types of companies are looked down upon by Wall Street. They are not part of the initial public offering (IPO) racket, are usually not as volatile and commission-generating as "hot" stocks, and more often than not are absent from the mergers and acquisitions (M&A)

market. They simply stick to their business and pay us, as owners, our fair share of the profits in cash. There's nothing wrong with that.

The Kimberly-Clark Corporation is a good example. Boring does not even begin to describe Kimberly. This company makes Kleenex tissue, Scott and Cottonelle toilet paper, Huggies, Little Swimmers Diapers, and Kotex and Poise products for women. And some of you now—and more of you later—will be familiar with another of their brands, Depend. Go out to dinner or stay in a hotel, and you'll see more dull Kimberly products in the kitchens and restrooms. Should you have to visit a doctor or the hospital, you will find a large and growing number of Kimberly products there: gloves, gowns, masks, booties, scrubs, and the ever-attractive hairnets. Kimberly sells its products across the globe, and about half of its sales come from outside the United States. Sales have been growing at a compound annual growth rate of 4.9% for the past five years. Operating profit has risen at a rate of 3.4% in the same period. Net income per share is up the same 4.9% as sales. Ho-hum. . . . Dividend growth in the same period is a positive 8.0%, as the company's payout ratio has risen modestly from 45% to 55%. And Kimberly has paid a dividend continuously since 1930 and raised it every year since 1972.

Now Kimberly is a business and is subject to all sorts of volatility. Input costs, primarily pulp and energy, can move around a lot. Competition with Procter & Gamble, Georgia-Pacific, and SCA in Europe can affect near-term results. Kimberly has some chinks in its armor, most notably its European operations and the overall tissue business. But when all is said and done, it's a well-established, stable business with clear if modest growth prospects. Around 50% of the profits come back to investors in the form of a check.

Despite its clear attributes, Kimberly is viewed by the stock market as a lesser company, not a "grower," and therefore trades at a relatively low valuation. That low price and the high dividend, currently $2.64 on an annual basis or $0.66 per quarter, translate into a very attractive 4.0% yield—twice that of the broader U.S. market. Combine that with the quality of the payment—representing only a little more than half of net income and a little less than half of FCF—and dividend growth prospects of 5.0%–7.0% over the next five years, and the cash return profile would seem pretty attractive.

Not to Wall Street. Wall Street wants action, wants M&A, wants lots of turnover. Kimberly offers none of these. Instead, on February 23, 2010, the board of directors at Kimberly raised the dividend by 10% and thereby signaled their assessment of the company's fundamental strength and outlook. Unlike earnings or guidance, a dividend can't be faked. One week after the company raised its cash distribution by 10%, a leading Wall Street brokerage lowered its rating on the shares of Kimberly-Clark to "sell" from "neutral." The reasoning was simple: there were risks of near-term, negative revisions to "consensus" earnings estimates—a key prop in Wall Street's internal theater of the absurd—due to rising pulp costs. The brokerage lowered its 12-month "target price" (another of the props) from $63 to $60. At the time, the shares were trading at $61. Two weeks later, the same brokerage added Kimberly to its "Conviction Sell" list, a gathering place for the worst of the worst, at least in the eyes of that brokerage. The analyst once again lowered his published earnings estimates for the near-in years and adjusted his "target price" down a whopping 5.0% to $57. The shares were still trading at that time at $60.

So on one hand, a company raises its cash payment to company owners by 10%. On the other hand, a Wall Street brokerage that makes money from trading stocks recommends that investors sell their shares out of concern that the price may drop all of 5.0%. It's no surprise that we will choose the increased cash payment and ignore the near-term noise. We run a business, and the purpose of that business is to generate high and rising cash distributions for our clients. We're not here to support the trading activity of a Wall Street brokerage. How did things work out? On July 25, 2010, four months after rating Kimberly a Conviction Sell, the brokerage reversed course and removed the shares from the penalty box. The analyst wrote that the near-term, negative earnings pressures had not materialized. He raised his earnings estimates and target price back to previous levels.[2] It makes your head spin.

While on the Conviction Sell list, the Kimberly shares rose 6.6% versus a decline for the S&P 500 Index of 3.5%, a difference of 10% in just four months. Even against a benchmark of peers, the S&P 500 Consumer Staples Index, Kimberly outperformed by 6.0% in the same period. Longer term, the same is true: as we've seen over and over again, the tortoise whips the hare and does so handily. Over a 10-year period, Kimberly beats the market by 5.3% per year. Over a 20-year period, the advantage is 1.7% per year. For 30 years, the difference is just shy of 4.0% per year. So how does dividend investing differ from stock investing? It focuses on the long-term determinants of value—the dividend and dividend growth—and ignores the near-term, turnover-for-turnover's-sake advice of Wall Street.

The final irony is that several months later, Kimberly did succumb to higher input costs and competitive pressure and "missed" a quarter. The stock fell 5.0%, albeit from the $66 level. That's the trouble with trying to work the casino with the "help" of the brokerages. Not only do you have to count on them to get the near-term business issues correct, but also to guess as to when and how other market participants will react to the same information. Good luck with that.

Sectors and Diversification

Locating individual securities and even entire sectors with an attractive profile can be very satisfying, but it is not the same as managing a dividend portfolio in a prudent manner. That requires diversifying the dividend sources so that the investor's income stream is insulated to the extent possible from a single company having to or choosing to cut its dividend. The events of 2008 and 2009, when the entire bank sector—traditionally a rich source of dividends—was stripped clean of its distributions stand as a clear lesson on the perils of not diversifying. Yet the structure of the U.S. stock market as represented in the S&P 500 Index makes it hard to do so. It is divided into 10 different sectors, but the number and weighting are quite arbitrary, particularly when compared to the opportunity set from the perspective of the dividend investor.

As you can see from Figure 5.1, the S&P 500 Index as currently constituted accords only 11% to the consumer staples sector on the basis of market capitalization, but that sector represents more than 18% of the aggregate dividends available to investors in those same 500 companies. The situation is the same in telecommunications. It represents 8.6% of the dividend opportunity—and has very high yields—but just 2.7% of the market. Financials and information technology are characterized by lots of securities and low yields. They are the two biggest sectors of the "stock" market but are far less significant parts of the dividend market. (To make matters worse, the S&P 500 Index no longer includes American Depository Receipts (ADRs) of major global corporations, a significant source of dividend income, as we will discuss shortly.) As dividend investors, we seek to diversify across the dividend-paying opportunities of the public equity

FIGURE 5.1   S&P 500 Index Dividend Weighted Versus Market Cap Weighted (sector weights and dividend yields)

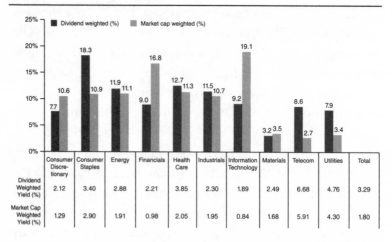

	Consumer Discre-tionary	Consumer Staples	Energy	Financials	Health Care	Industrials	Information Technology	Materials	Telecom	Utilities	Total
Dividend Weighted Yield (%)	2.12	3.40	2.88	2.21	3.85	2.30	1.89	2.49	6.68	4.76	3.29
Market Cap Weighted Yield (%)	1.29	2.90	1.91	0.98	2.05	1.95	0.84	1.68	5.91	4.30	1.80

Source: FactSet Research Systems, April 2010.

markets. But just because there is a materials sector (all of 3.2%–3.5% of both the stock market and dividend market) doesn't mean you need to own materials stocks in a dividend portfolio. Given the low yields and business volatility typical of materials companies, owning them in a dividend portfolio goes beyond diversification to outright contradiction of the strategy. Consumer discretionary and information technology are much the same. Yes, they exist and appear to be quite large in the stock market, but you do not have to invest in them as part of an income-oriented strategy when yields there are so low and so uncertain. We often see competitive equity income products that play "by the rules" and own stocks in all 10 "GIC" sectors, as they are known. They do so at a cost of lowering their yield and increasing their volatility.

There are exceptions and companies that could become exceptions. Within consumer discretionary, McDonald's might as well be considered a staple for the role that it plays in U.S. and global culture. In recent years the company has shifted from growth at all costs to profitability and has increased its dividend to a level equating to a 50% payout in the most recent year. Walmart could be dividend stock. Yes, you heard me right, Walmart. To paraphrase the old Kmart announcement, "Attention Walmart board members! It's time to raise the payout from the current low level around 30%." Even Sam Walton would approve. He reinvested every penny as he grew the business, but now Walmart has won, and it's time to start enjoying the benefits of ample distributable cash. Home Depot is not too far behind. The rest of the consumer discretionary space is littered with fly-by-night (a few years) operations, or ones with such tenuous and volatile profitability that they rightly do not pay a significant dividend. (Airline stocks are a great example.) They exist for the benefit of the near-term speculator. Investors need not bother with them, at least not as part of their core portfolio.

The much heralded information technology sector is in a similar situation. Very few of the names exist for the dividend investor in the sense that the components of return in becoming a partial owner of the company are dominated by cash payments. But like the consumer discretionary sector, there are some mature, cash-generative companies whose management teams are coming to the realization that reinvesting all their profits has already or will soon generate incrementally diminishing returns. A few more years of such returns and they could come to the conclusion that paying a high dividend isn't such a bad thing after all. I've already mentioned Microsoft and Intel as companies moving in that direction. Time will tell which other tech firms join their ranks.

Add it all up, and the industry standard benchmark S&P 500 Index is rather remote from the dividend universe. One notable consequence of this variance is that the total return performance of a committed dividend portfolio will rarely coincide with the performance of the S&P 500. How could it? The overlap is limited. That is, in any given year, the total return of a dividend strategy may be well ahead of the broader market or well behind, but it will rarely be exactly in line. Over the long term, the tortoise beats the hare and does so handily, but at any given point in the race, they are unlikely to be side-by-side. In the race as it is currently run, the tortoise will almost always have the "inside" lane. When the stock market is up sharply, usually led by the most volatile—read non-dividend sectors such as consumer discretionary, materials, and technology—a committed dividend portfolio will almost certainly underperform, at least initially. Conversely, on the way down or in a market moving sideways, the dividend portfolio will likely outperform the alternative that has little or no yield floor. This is another way of expressing the fact that dividend portfolios will have lower volatility than ones that don't benefit from having a significant component of their return coming from cash. If you like watching your stock portfolio jump around with every bit of news, don't invest in this style. It will bore you mightily.

Foreign Dividends

To compensate for the relative paucity of dividends in the U.S. market, investors can and should access dividend streams in the major foreign markets of Europe, where the attributes that we prize remain available. Indeed, in contrast to what has happened to the United States over the past 25 years, investors and corporate management teams in the United Kingdom in particular have remained oriented toward dividends as the central component of total return. For example, take a look at the following recent statement from Scottish & Southern Energy (SSE), a U.K. utility: SSE "takes a longer-term view and believes that profit is a means to an end: sustained real growth in the dividend, the delivery of which is its first responsibility to shareholders."[3] In an ideal world, the dividend investor's entire portfolio would consist of companies espousing such a view.

Yield and Payout

With the inclination box checked at many non-U.S. corporations, it should not come as a surprise that payout ratios and market yields are higher in most developed markets outside the United States (see Figure 5.2). (The difference in interest rates for government securities in various countries also plays an important role.) Compared to the U.S. market cash return of less than 2.0%, the FTSE 100 Index currently yields more than 3.0%. Most of the major markets in Europe are at or above that level. Canada is a bit lower; Australia rather higher. Only Japan has a market yield less than that of the United States. In terms of payout ratio, the U.S. market defines the low end of the range.

From the perspective of the dividend investor, many global firms that happen to be domiciled in Western Europe offer a good combination of dividend yield and dividend growth. Royal Dutch Shell (RDS) does the same thing that Exxon (XOM) does, but it pays company owners a good deal more. The difference in yield, 5.0%–6.0%, versus a dividend yield that is less than 3.0%, plus the fact that the RDS shares are

FIGURE 5.2   Global Dividend Payouts and Dividend Yields

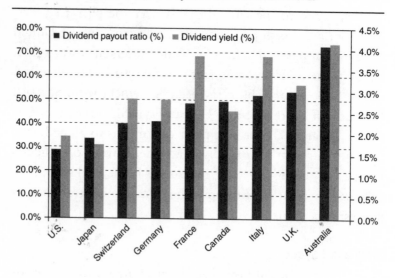

Source: Bloomberg Finance, LP, 2010.

readily accessible to U.S. investors as ADRs, makes them highly attractive to dividend investors.

Total Return

The math works the same in mature foreign markets as it does in the United States. *Dividends dominate the components of total return.* Higher-yielding securities outperform the lower and non-dividend securities, and of course, the broader market (see Table 5.1).

Just to offset the basic yield bias in these results, let me present another analysis in Table 5.2 that highlights the combined role of dividend yield and dividend growth. It comes courtesy of Société Générale Cross Asset Research and looks at the returns of the leading international markets from 1971 through 2009. It uses rolling 10-year average returns to smooth out volatility due to near-term investor preferences.

TABLE 5.1 International Returns by Dividend Quintile

		Australia	Canada	France	Germany	Japan	Switzerland	United Kingdom
Annual Total Return (%)								
	Universe	11.23	10.04	10.61	9.29	−0.38	12.53	8.94
Dividend Yield Quintile	Highest Yield	12.97	14.22	18.11	15.49	6.66	14.18	11.47
	High Yield	12.53	10.67	12.37	9.69	0.76	11.78	9.54
	Medium Yield	9.34	9.93	6.83	8.65	−2.12	11.48	8.61
	Low Yield	8.03	7.80	6.22	6.97	−6.29	4.73	6.75
	No Div	7.65	7.21	2.17	−1.38	−7.10	10.42	3.27

Non-U.S., developed markets; largest 1,000 stocks; equal-weighted returns; country neutral; rebalanced monthly; 12/31/1987–12/31/2009. Data from FactSet Research Systems, 2010.

TABLE 5.2 Dividends Dominate Developed Market Total Return (1981–2009)

Nominal Returns (%)

Return Component	United Kingdom	France	Germany	Australia	Canada	Japan	United States
Dividend yield	4.3	3.5	2.8	4.3	3.1	1.5	3.3
Dividend growth	7.1	7.0	4.9	8.4	6.4	2.1	4.6
Multiple expansion	0.2	−0.2	−0.2	−2.2	0.8	2.4	1.6
Total annualized returns	11.9	10.5	7.6	10.6	10.5	6.1	9.7

Real returns (%)

Return component	United Kingdom	France	Germany	Australia	Canada	Japan	United States
Dividend yield	4.3	3.5	2.8	4.3	3.1	1.5	3.3
Dividend growth	0.4	2.7	1.9	2.2	1.7	−0.9	0.5
Multiple expansion	0.2	−0.2	−0.2	−2.2	0.8	2.4	1.6
Total annualized returns	5.0	6.1	4.6	4.3	5.7	3.0	5.5

Source: Société Générale Cross Asset Research, 2010. Factors geometrically linked.

In the United States (and Japan) total return has been boosted by multiple expansion—stocks becoming more expensive during the height of the equity boom—but even in those cases, the dividends still dominate the equation. That is true whether or not you consider the returns in nominal terms or adjusted for inflation. (Japan is the only real exception, but keep in mind that Japan for many years has had abnormally low interest rates, which serve to boost valuation multiples.)

Not Foreign, But Global

Many of the large, dividend-oriented foreign companies are notable in that, although their stocks are listed in a relatively small country such as the United Kingdom, they are global businesses and offer a geographical diversification of income streams. Indeed, many of them are a good deal less "foreign" than they appear at first glance in that they derive a large portion of their revenue and profits from the United States. U.K.-listed companies such as GlaxoSmithKline, Unilever, and Diageo, which generate a third to a half of their sales in the United States, are good examples. In some sectors, it would be difficult not to go global as part of a dividend strategy. We generally tap into income streams of mature companies. When you consider that consolidation goes hand-in-hand with the shift to higher payouts, you realize that in sectors such as integrated energy and pharmaceuticals, for instance, the list of U.S.-based names is rather short. In those sectors, the stocks of global corporations headquartered outside the U.S. but available to U.S. investors as ADRs can play a helpful role in meeting a portfolio's demand for diversified income. Rather like the division of the stock market into 10 quite arbitrarily defined sectors, the separation between domestic ("safe and transparent") and foreign ("risky and opaque") is artificial at best. Indeed, the last two stock market crashes had their roots right here at home.

But the more important point is that globalization really has occurred. And the distinction between U.S.-distributed profits and non-U.S.-distributed profits is just not very meaningful anymore. Unilever could just as easily be called Best-foods, a large U.S. food company purchased by Unilever and headquartered in Engelwood Cliffs, New Jersey. Is it really a U.K. stock? It isn't particularly focused on the United Kingdom. Instead, it produces and markets food and personal care items all over the globe. According to Unilever, 2 billion people each day use its products, which are sold in 170 countries around the globe. And it recently started paying its dividend quarterly, like most dividend-paying U.S. companies.

The global sourcing of dividends works in both directions. Many iconic U.S. corporations such as Coca-Cola, Heinz, and McDonald's now derive half or more of their distributable profits from outside the United States. When clients sometimes raise their concern about having foreign-listed companies in the portfolio, I ask them whether they feel Coca-Cola—which makes most of its profits outside the United States—should be removed as a risky foreign entity. Generally the answer is no.

We do live in a global world. Diversifying the source of our dividend payments beyond just U.S.-listed companies to locations where yields, liquidity, and accounting standards are acceptable is a prudent course of action for the dividend investor. Note that the foreign markets of interest are by and large the mature ones of Western Europe. Emerging market stocks take themselves out of the equation because as "growth" vehicles, they rarely have attractive dividends. Even if they did, limited liquidity for Main Street U.S. investors, opaque accounting, and weak corporate governance limit investment opportunities. If you wish to "play" emerging markets other than through Coca-Cola and Unilever and similar global businesses that benefit from the high levels of economic activity in those corners of the world, feel free to do so, but not as part of a core dividend-generating strategy.

Not all foreign markets are alike. Though considered mature and generally safe from an accounting and corporate governance perspective, Japan and Switzerland, for instance, are simply not very fertile for the dividend investor. Both countries have had low interest rates for a very long period of time, and with the cost of the risk-free government alternative so low, companies have not had to offer a competitive yield to attract capital. By the same measure, some so-called emerging markets can be of interest, at least for institutional investors who can purchase the local shares. (The American Depository Receipts [ADRs], which U.S. retail investors can buy easily, may be illiquid or simply unavailable.) For instance, both Brazil and Taiwan offer opportunities to generate significant cash returns and are notable in that though they are considered emerging, they have been so categorized for decades. In fact, many of their companies and industries are quite mature and cash generative.

Taxes

When looking at non-U.S.-listed companies, taxes matter. Most (but not all) foreign governments withhold a portion of dividend payments to U.S. investors, generally 15%. Depending on how you are investing (mutual fund, managed account, etc.), you may be able to reclaim the withholding and get it in cash with a several-month delay or more practically, just use it as a credit against taxes payable to the United States. Consult your tax advisor or investment platform to learn how foreign dividends are handled from a tax perspective.

In the meantime, you should know that U.K.-listed companies generally do not withhold anything from the declared
dividend payments to U.S. investors. That's one more reason
why we like to invest in global businesses headquartered in
the United Kingdom. When we look at comparable investments, with one based in the United Kingdom and the other
in a "15% withholding" market, we may go with the non-
U.K. name, but we would take into account the 15% hair-
cut that the non-U.K. alternative would incur. At the other
end of the spectrum, there are countries such as Switzerland
that add the insult of high withholding (35%) to the injury of
very low yields. In theory, 20% of the Swiss withholding is
reclaimable (to get back to the net withholding of 15%), but
the process can be cumbersome and take years. Switzerland
is simply not attractive for the U.S.-based dividend investor.
Some other countries, such as Australia, don't withhold tax
on dividends to foreign investors as long as the company has
paid its full share of corporate taxes. In those cases, the dividend is considered "franked," and we get the full payment.
It's an enlightened policy that our own country would do well
to emulate. We still owe tax on the income, even if franked,
to the U.S. government, but at least the money does not have
to make an intermediate stop.

Special Dividends

Special dividends are a final reason to look abroad in a dividend portfolio. Foreign companies will pay them as a means
of distributing excess but perhaps unsustainable cash flows,
say from the sale of a business or a particularly robust period
of operations. Over the years, our investors have benefited
from these occasional and unpredictable payments. We don't
count on them or forecast them, but welcome them all the
same. Remember, the return from a dividend is always posi-

tive, and we admire a company's management that recognizes that there will be times when the best thing to do with a windfall is to simply send it on to the owners of the company.

Special dividends used to be much more frequent in this country, but in Trader Nation, the practice has become rare. It is an exception that again shows how different dividend investing can be from regular stock speculation. My own employer, Federated Investors (FII), is a good example. It paid large, special dividends in 2008 and 2010. According to traditional stock market thinking, family-controlled companies such as Federated often trade at a "discount" to their industry peers that are not family controlled and can therefore more easily participate in M&A. That is, family control is viewed negatively. From a dividend investor's perspective, however, the opposite may be true. Family-controlled companies often have a lot of family members counting on that dividend. While you as a nonfamily member may not have full voting rights, you generally get the same dividend as the cousin and the aunt. At least in this regard—and it is the most important regard—your interests are aligned with the controlling family. Family control on its own means nothing. The underlying business still has to be able to generate excess cash flows, but if it does, having a long list of relatives clipping their coupons can work to your benefit.

Exchange Traded Funds (ETFs)

As you work your way with your advisor through these options—getting the right balance of yield and growth, sector exposure, foreign stocks, and so forth—the issue of ETFs is bound to come up. Given the clear attraction of investing in dividends but the real-world challenge of actually sorting through the good and the bad, some investors might decide to invest in a broad array of stock market dividends in the form of a dividend-oriented ETF. ETFs are the follow-on products to the wildly popular index funds that emerged during the 1980s and 1990s. During that period, the low-cost, "passive" structures handily outperformed actively managed mutual funds. Now that index funds have evolved to offer specific variants, such as a focus on high-dividend securities, and they charge quite low fees, some investors wonder whether they might be a better way to go. Though this strategy holds some merit, it is far from clear that it is the best option.

A rising tide lifts all boats, and the two-decade bull market from 1982 to 2000 offered an almost perfect environment for low-cost, passively managed products. The subsequent decade has shown the opposite. Hugging the stock market from 2000 to 2009 would have meant getting flat returns. Your active manager had at least a chance to do much better than that. The same logic holds in regard to dividend-focused ETFs. You pay lower fees than a traditional, actively managed portfolio, but you are basically getting a "dumb" product that is more likely to be reactive than proactive. It will have no way to answer the question about "the ability and inclination of management to pay and increase the dividend over the next three to five years." So it will either include very high-yielding but at-risk securities, or if it applies certain blanket measures to reduce that risk (such as a low payout ratio), the yield will also be reduced and the reliance on the stock market will increase. For all their flaws, dividend-oriented ETFs should still do better than the broader, dividend-starved market over long measurement periods, but ETF investors take on the risk of being "penny wise and pound foolish" by assuming that they are superior to an actively managed dividend product, particularly in uncertain economic times when it literally pays to have people monitoring the businesses that you own.

Dividend Reinvestment

Let me end this section on a high note about the not-so-secret power of dividend reinvestment. You have probably already observed that in regard to dividend reinvestment, every single investment guide and professional advisor is singing from the same page of the hymnal, and for good reason. Dividend reinvestment is probably the most powerful tool for wealth creation available to the retail investor, and you don't have to do a thing to benefit from it other than actually own dividend-paying securities. The math of dividend reinvestment is exceptionally compelling. Take two portfolios, each with $10,000 in initial capital and both with the same annual return of 10%. The first portfolio gets to the 10% market with a 5% dividend yield and 5% dividend growth reflected in capital appreciation. (Remember from earlier that whether or not you take the dividends will affect your asset level but will have no impact whatsoever on your measured total return for any given period. Those are two, very separate phenomena.) After 30 years, the capital in the 5 + 5 portfolio has grown to $43,219 and the investor has collected $33,219 in coupons. Not bad. But if the dividends were reinvested to increase the capital base further, it gets much, much better. After 30 years, the capital has grown to $174,494. At that point, say you had retired and were looking for income, the same portfolio would be generating $8,725 per year, almost as much as the initial investment, each and every year. Retirement accounts such as 401(k)s are designed to allow investors to realize the benefits of dividend reinvestment: you usually don't have access to the money that you are setting aside until you are ready to retire, and the activity in the account is not taxed until you start taking distributions.

There's really only one trick in regard to dividend reinvestment: you have to have dividends for it to work. Fill your retirement account with non-dividend-paying stocks or low-yielding equity funds, and you deprive yourself of what is, in effect, an automatic wealth-production mechanism. In the second, stock-appreciation-only portfolio, you would be in the same position in regard to overall capital, but as shown in Chapter 2 the stock market hares have a hard time keeping up with the tortoises, particularly for the long haul. Their total return often ends up being several hundred basis points (several percent) lower than that of the dividend securities. That translates into much lower asset levels over a 30-year investment period.

Conclusion

Outlook

Did the financial crisis and the ensuing stock market crash of 2008 put an end to the worst abuses of Trader Nation? Has the 25-year period of cheap money, perceived low risk, and high turnover come to an end? I can't say for certain, but I can rely on the tendency seen throughout nature and society to revert to the mean. From a dividend perspective, the last 25 years have represented a significant deviation from the normal risk and return characteristics in the equity markets. So the question becomes: what is the likelihood that the present environment of low interest rates, low equity risk premiums, and frequent trading is sustained or accentuated even further versus the probability that our capital markets revert to a situation where money costs something, equities are thought to carry some risk, and therefore company owners and managers skew the return pattern toward cash payments? I know which side I'm on, but timing reversion to the mean is very difficult. It could happen tomorrow or a decade from now, but it will happen, and investors and traders should not be surprised when it does.

For those of you who don't want to stand around waiting for the Godot of mean reversion (but it really is coming), the near-term outlook for dividend-oriented securities is equally good. The market's sharp rally in 2009—led by lower-quality and non-dividend or low-yielding issues—created a bad-news-is-good-news scenario. Because the market yield is once again so low, a high-quality dividend portfolio will have little difficulty besting the broader market from these levels (if held for at least a few years). So if you want to be able to say that you "beat the market" and most of your neighbors, then now is an excellent time to invest for dividends.

On an absolute basis, which is all investors should really care about, the situation is nearly as bright. That's because the United States is facing more modest rates of growth over the next decade as businesses and consumers operate with less cheap debt. Some companies will appropriately reinvest profits in emerging markets, but the general landscape is one in which corporate payouts to company owners ought to rise. That would reverse the trend noted earlier of corporate payouts falling from around 50% of net income to just 30% in recent years. At the same time, more and more baby boomers will be retiring and shifting toward an income focus from their investments. On both the business front and from investors, supply and demand will work in favor of companies returning to more normal dividend payout regimes. If you recall, I started this overview with the observation that a market with a 2.0% yield (what we have now) means less than 30% of the value of the S&P 500 Index is received in current dividend payments extended into the future, and that the remaining 70% plus is in the form of expected growth of those payments. Were the market to move back toward a more "normal" 4.0% yield—a notion that would strike most market participants as inconceivable—through the combination of modest profit growth and a return to higher payout levels, dividend investors would have a much easier time justifying the market's current price. About 56% of the S&P 500 Index's price at that time would be covered by the income from the dividend alone. That's a good deal more comfortable and realistic than the situation today. The far less attractive alternative is getting to a 4.0% cash return the hard way, through investors cutting the market in half until it is appropriately priced for its cash payments.

When the pendulum does swing back, what will the equity markets look like? The dividend investor can appear naive and simplistic in the face of the "real," rumble-tumble world of equities, and I don't imagine that stocks would appreciate or depreciate only when a dividend was raised or cut. Claiming that the markets should trade perfectly around dividend information would be just another version of the efficient-market hypothesis (EMH). That is hardly the case. Nevertheless, market volatility would necessarily diminish. For most U.S. companies, dividends are declared and paid quarterly. The level is reset once a year, although companies are free to reset it each and every quarter. The simple fact is that long-term distributable cash flows from large, publicly owned companies don't vary much day to day. So the present value—the price you might be willing to pay for those dividend streams—should not swing around too much either.

Still, the equity markets will remain a volatile place. For any number of reasons, there will always be more buyers than sellers one day, and the reverse will be true the next. Movement of cash in and out of the market from other asset classes will continue to make share prices jump around. For instance, though we often go months without making a fundamental trade in our dividend portfolios, every day we have new inflows or outflows of cash as our clients come and go. That means we are constantly buying and selling the shares of the companies in the portfolios, at least in small measure.

Almost as frequently there will be new information in the marketplace that some participants might choose to interpret as affecting dividend growth and therefore the appropriate price of a security. Investors will get some of those decisions right and some wrong, but either way, there would be activity.

Speculation is and would remain an integral part of free markets. It serves the purpose of allocating capital to high-risk ventures as well as providing room for "differences of opinion" as to the outlook of individual businesses, sectors, and the entire market. As such, there would still be "growth" stocks and "deep value" stocks and early-stage companies (all with no or minimal dividends), but investors would appreciate that they are speculators, not investors, when they owned and traded these securities. And these stocks would trade with the degree of risk properly reflected in their price. The primary difference in the marketplace would be one of scale. Instead of having two-thirds of the public equity market issues offering little or no dividends, the opposite would be true. The vast majority of stocks would be priced somewhere around the expected present value of their future dividend payments. That is not a very radical notion.

The Challenge

Perhaps the biggest challenge in getting investors to focus on stocks as platforms for dividend distribution is a mental one. It is to reintroduce to the investing public, after more than 25 years of desuetude, the key concept that frames our view of the market: income *is* total return. Say it loudly, say it proudly, say it to your financial advisor. The earlier section decomposing total returns into their components—dominated by the dividend—shows it clearly, but the industry is set up to view capital appreciation and income as separate forms of activity, with the latter too often being reserved for the elderly, the dim-witted, and the scared, while growth products are foisted on the young and aggressive. That's ironic because the merits of dividend investing are probably greatest for the young investor who doesn't immediately need to take the income and can therefore compound the benefits of a dividend-focused strategy by reinvesting the cash payments.

As a consequence of the artificial separation of the components of total return into income and capital appreciation, too many investors have become accustomed to seeing income coming solely from instruments such as corporate bonds, municipal obligations, Treasuries, and certificates of deposit. They are not comfortable with the idea that income can come from stocks where the prices jump around daily. Yes, it is true that stock prices are far more volatile than those of bonds and other fixed-income securities, and that there is more risk to the coupon and the invested capital in the case of stocks, but a well-diversified portfolio of high-yielding, dividend-growing equities goes a long way to mitigating that risk. In the present very-low-interest-rate environment, investors need to see equities once again, as they were in the past, as a source of income, current income to help them meet their immediate needs if they are taking the distributions out of the portfolio or the income that generates superior asset growth if they can reinvest dividends. That mental block has to be overcome. Up until the early 1980s, equities were more widely viewed in this manner, and it is my belief that they will again become perfectly valid and acceptable forms of income generation.

Let me conclude by making one final reference to Benjamin Graham: approach your investments as you would your business, soberly, with an eye toward the long term, and from a cash return perspective. And take the stock out of the equation. Focus instead on the checks in the mail. If they keep coming and rise gradually—or if your ownership stake keeps expanding due to dividend reinvestment—then the value of the portfolio will be just fine. A critic well schooled in behavioral finance would note here how unlikely it is that the average investor can restrain his or her passions and follow the straight and narrow path of dividend investing for decades on end—and the critic would be right. Most of the individuals visiting the race track or casino pretty much know that they are going to lose money, but they go all the same. As I noted at the beginning of the book, a measure of irrational behavior is part of the human condition. Against that backdrop, dividend investing does not require the strict discipline of a cloistered monk.

Go ahead, speculate, play the numbers, work the casino, buy those Chilean copper futures, trade those penny stocks, get in on the tech IPOs, buy and sell frequently. It is always exciting, it can be fun, and it might even be profitable. But it is not investment, and it should not make up more than a small fraction of your retirement assets. Perhaps up to 5% of your portfolio can be risked in that type of behavior. If you are a Rockefeller or a Gates, you can afford to risk more; if not, you probably ought to limit the speculation to not much more than the "spare change" that is in your brokerage or retirement account.

But the temptation to gamble can be nearly irresistible. I can't help but note that the online brokerages are again taking out full-page newspaper advertisements and are now offering equity trades for just $8. It's like they are giving it away! It's similar to a casino putting out a sign that free drinks are available inside. But by encouraging you to trade rather than invest, the $8 price is no bargain. In fact, it is a false economy; you'll lose much more by trading frequently at $8 than by abstaining from all but the most necessary transactions. Keynes's suggestion of a transfer tax on stocks again comes to mind, but we live in a free society, and people must be allowed to act against their own self-interest. "The fault, dear Brutus, is not in the stars, but in ourselves. . . ." Spare yourself that agony that comes with poring over the latest brokerage research or a hot stock newsletter. You will get much more from life from Shakespeare, from Twain, from Dickens and Dostoevsky. Spend your free time reading them, and your dividend-focused portfolio will do just fine.

Afterword

(Death and) Taxes

The financial services industry operates in a pretax environment, at least in regard to presenting product performance, while you and I and most investors inhabit a posttax world. Given the critical importance (and high level) of taxation for most stock investors, you would rightly expect a commentary on taxes to be integral to laying out an investment strategy. And in your discussions with your financial planner or broker, it very much ought to be. But the tax outlook is currently so uncertain and changes so frequently that I've set it off here as an afterword.

While I am comfortable arguing that dividend payout ratios and the market's yield are likely to increase over the next decade—positive developments for dividend investors—I have no such good news when it comes to the taxes that investors will have to pay on those dividends. Historically, dividends have been viewed by the IRS as a form of income and have usually been taxed at the individual's marginal income tax rate. In contrast, capital gains have traditionally been viewed as a separate form of investment return and have had a different, generally lower, specified tax rate. Since 2003, the tax rates on long-term capital gains and on dividend income have been equalized at 15%. Bravo. That equal and low treatment was set to expire at the end of 2010, but, as this book goes to print, it has been extended for another two years. Nevertheless, investors should brace themselves for the possibility (indeed likelihood) that taxes on dividend income will increase at some point in the next several years. The real question for dividend investors will be whether the rates on dividends and capital gains will go up by the same amount or whether dividends will again suffer a tax disadvantage. Time will tell, but I do want to point out here that even if unequal levels of taxation are reinstated, the total return advantage that dividend-oriented securities enjoy over a stock-price-dominated strategy is unlikely to be reversed, even on an after-tax basis. It is simply too large.

Consider, for example, two investments that generate a 10% annual total return. One is from a dividend-oriented portfolio that generates half its annual return from the coupon and half from capital appreciation. The other portfolio offers no income, just stock price appreciation in the amount of 10%. Table A.1 and Table A.2 show the after-tax return in a variety of scenarios. The most punitive one—with the greatest gap between the tax on capital gains and the tax on ordinary income—is highlighted in bold and amounts to a maximum after-tax advantage for the stock-only portfolio of 100 basis points (1.0%) at a 20% tax rate differential for a one-year period. The maximum penalty is far smaller than the typical gap (which we noted earlier was several percent) between the long-term performance of the dividend-oriented portfolios and non-dividend portfolios.

**TABLE A.1   After-Tax Rate of Return on a Pretax Total Return of 10%
(all stock price appreciation; no dividend component)**

Capital Gains Tax Rate		
20.0%	30.0%	40.0%
8.0%	7.5%	7.0%

**TABLE A.2   After-Tax Rate of Return on a Pretax Total Return of 10%
(half from dividend income and half from stock price appreciation)**

		Capital Gains Tax Rate		
		20%	30%	40%
Marginal dividend tax rate	20%	8.0%	7.5%	7.0%
	30%	7.5%	7.0%	6.5%
	40%	**7.0%**	6.5%	6.0%

If held for longer time periods, the capital gains portfolio will show an additional benefit from the compounding of gains whose taxation is deferred until final sale. That will serve to widen the gap with the mixed portfolio where a taxable event is occurring regularly. Still, the fact that taxes are likely to go up, and that dividends are taxed twice and highly, does not make up for the long-term total return advantages that a dividend-focused portfolio can offer. Past performance is, as the warning goes, not a guarantee of future returns, but with most signals pointing in the direction of dividends, and only the prospect of a differential tax rate standing in the way, the outlook for dividend investing remains compelling.

While the math of double and differential taxation of dividends may be punitive, in the real world, it may not matter. It seems improbable that stock market valuations are going to change dramatically due to new tax rates on dividends. Is Grandma really going to sell all her utility, telco, and consumer staple stocks because the tax rate is going up? It's not likely. And as managers of dividend-focused portfolios, we're not likely to either. In fact, with roughly one-half of equity assets in retirement or other tax-shielded structures, it's not clear that a change in the tax rate will have much of an impact on investor demand for dividend stocks. More generally, there doesn't seem to be much evidence that the market takes into account changing tax rates in determining valuations. There are just too many other factors that come into play.

The greatest impact were rates to move higher may not be on the market itself, but on corporate behavior. Imagine yourself as the treasurer of a large corporation that is trying to determine what to do with the excess cash that it is accumulating. As you formulate a recommendation to the board of directors, you would certainly take into account the tax consequences for shareholders of increasing the dividend versus using the cash for share repurchases (taxed as capital gains), mergers and acquisitions, or further investment in the business. In that analysis, you might rationally conclude that increasing the dividend should not be at the top of the list. Companies that are traditionally viewed as dividend payers (e.g., telcos, consumer staples, utilities) are not likely to be deterred from raising their dividends by those calculations, but companies on the periphery of the dividend world (e.g., the technology giants sitting on large cash reserves) could choose not to do so because of the prospective unfavorable taxation of dividends. In the end, the new rates may trim a point off of the expected dividend growth rate for the overall market, but it would likely come from those sectors where dividends have historically not been a high priority.

Endnotes

Chapter 1

1. The starting point is Charles P. Kindleberger, *Manias, Panics, and Crashes: A History of Financial Crises*, 3rd edition (New York: John Wiley & Sons, 1996). Note that Kindleberger's account is part of a broader debate among economists and market theorists about the nature of speculative bubbles and the necessity (or not) of lenders of last resort; it is not a narrative account of speculation. See also Edward Chancellor, *Devil Take the Hindmost: A History of Financial Speculation* (New York: Farrar, Straus and Giroux, 1999) for a more straightforward history of the topic.

2. John Burr Williams, *The Theory of Investment Value* (Cambridge: Harvard University Press, 1938), p. 3.

3. Williams, *The Theory of Investment Value*, pp. 33–34.

4. John Maynard Keynes, *The General Theory of Employment, Interest, and Money* (London: Macmillan and Co., 1936), pp. 155–156.

5. Benjamin Graham, *The Intelligent Investor*, revised 1973 edition, edited by Jason Zweig (New York: Harper Collins, 2003), p. 18.

6. Graham, *The Intelligent Investor*, p. 523.

7. FactSet Research Systems, data as of December 27, 2010.

8. Sanford C. Bernstein & Co., LLC, October 2010.

9. Ned Davis Research, Inc, 2010.

10. Robert Shiller database, Yale University, http://www.econ.yale .edu/~shiller/data.htm. Cowles Commission data from 1871 to 1926; S&P 500 precursor data (sometimes referred to as the Ibbotson data series) from 1926 to 1957; S&P 500 Index data from 1957.

11. Robert Shiller database, Yale University, http://www.econ.yale .edu/~shiller/data.htm. A note on attribution methodology: The percentage derived from dividends is calculated by subtracting the capital appreciation portion from the total return measure. This simple arithmetic step appears to be the standard method by which the financial services industry comes up with the oft-quoted 40%–50% figure. The second step used here is to then subtract the dividend growth metric from the capital appreciation figure. What is left is capital appreciation independent of dividends—just 9% of the annual total return from 1871 and 11% from 1926. Returns more properly ought to be decomposed geometrically (using division rather than subtraction). Because a geometric decomposition introduces an interaction effect, the amount explicitly tied to dividends falls slightly but the difference is insignificant.

12. Robert Arnott, "Dividends and the Three Dwarfs," Editor's Corner, *Financial Analysis Journal*, Vol. 59, No. 2 (March–April 2003).

13. Andrew Lapthorne, Société Générale, Cross Asset Research, Global Income Investor Report, 2010.

14. Williams, *The Theory of Investment Value*, p. 4.

15. Karl Marx, *Capital: A Critique of Political Economy*, Vol. 2 (Chicago: Kerr & Co., 1913), pp. 203–205.

16. Irving Fisher, *The Nature of Capital and Income* (New York: Augustus M. Kelley, 1965 reprint of 1906 original), pp. 188, 231.

17. Edgar Lawrence Smith, *Common Stocks as Long-Term Investments* (New York: MacMillan, 1928).

18. Williams, *The Theory of Investment Value*, p. 80. Myron Gordon simplified the analysis of Williams by inserting a constant

growth and discount rate into the equation. The resulting Gordon Growth Model has become a shorthand way of determining the present value of a dividend stream.

19. Graham and Dodd are discussed in greater detail in the section on value investing in Chapter 2.

20. Aswath Damodaran, *Investment Valuation* (New York: John Wiley & Sons, 1996), p. 191.

Chapter 2

1. Data set from 1979 through 2009. Source: FactSet Research Systems, 2010. Universe of 500 largest U.S. stocks; 50 top-yielding securities that also have 3-year dividend growth of greater than 5%, net cash flow from operations per share/dividends per share, not in the lowest quintile, 3-year stock price volatility not in the highest quintile, and debt/EBITDA, not in the highest quintile; equal-weighted returns.

2. Robert D. Arnott and Clifford S. Asness, "Surprise! Higher Dividends = Higher Earnings Growth," *Financial Analyst Journal,* January–February 2003, pp. 70–87 makes the direct assertion that higher payouts can lead to higher dividend growth.

3. Jason Zweig's comment in Graham's *The Intelligent Investor,* p. 506.

4. The large reported EPS in 2000 was the result of an extraordinary gain associated with the separation of Reynolds from RJR Nabisco. The large negative result in 2003 was due to goodwill and trademark impairment resulting from a write-down in the book value of numerous Reynolds cigarette brands, reflecting the industry's secular decline.

5. Benjamin Graham and David L. Dodd, along with Charles Tatham, Jr., *Security Analysis: Principles and Technique,* 3rd edition (New York: McGraw Hill, 1951), pp. 432–433.

6. Graham and Dodd, *Security Analysis,* p. 586.

7. Richard Bernstein and Lisa Kirschner, Richard Bernstein Advisors, LLC, September 2010.

8. Williams, *The Theory of Investment Value,* p. 57.

Chapter 3

1. Graham and Dodd, *Security Analysis*, p. 429.
2. Graham and Dodd, *Security Analysis*, p. 387.
3. Merton Miller and Franco Modigliani, "Dividend Policy, Growth & the Valuation of Shares," *Journal of Business*, Vol. XXXIV, No. 4 (October 1961), p. 428.
4. Miller and Modigliani, pp. 411–433.
5. Keynes, *General Theory*, p. 159.

Chapter 4

1. Stock Value = Dividend/(Discount Rate − Growth Rate). Solved for the Discount Rate (also known as the Required Rate of Return), it becomes Dividend Yield + Growth Rate.
2. Graham, *The Intelligent Investor*, p. 205.
3. As an exception, I must note Josh Peters, the editor of Morningstar's excellent *Dividend Investor* newsletter. If you opt for the go-it-alone path, you must at a minimum subscribe to it. Even if you more wisely choose to use a professional, reading the *Dividend Investor* is an efficient (not too time-consuming) and inexpensive way of staying on top of your portfolio and your financial advisor.

Chapter 5

1. Data as of June 20, 2010, for all companies mentioned in this section.
2. Goldman Sachs reports, March 1, March 16, July 18, July 25, 2010.
3. Scottish & Southern Energy, plc, financial report for the year to March 31, 2010. Issued May 19, 2010.

Suggestions for Further Review

Benjamin Graham, *The Intelligent Investor*; updated and with commentary by Jason Zweig. (New York: Harper Business Essentials, 2003). Originally published in 1949, this book underwent regular revision in subsequent decades.

Benjamin Graham and David Dodd, *Security Analysis* (New York: McGraw-Hill, 1934). Graham materially revised this work in subsequent editions.

John Maynard Keynes, *The General Theory of Employment, Interest and Money* (New York: Harcourt, Brace, 1936), especially Chapter 12.

Andrew Lapthorne, Albert Edwards, Dylan Grice, (and former colleague James Montier), Cross Asset Research, Société Générale.

Josh Peters, *The Morningstar Dividend Investor* newsletter.

Josh Peters, *The Ultimate Dividend Playbook* (Hoboken, NJ: Wiley, 2008).

Robert Shiller, *Irrational Exuberance* (Princeton: Princeton University Press, 2000).

Robert Shiller database, Yale University, http://www.econ.yale.edu/~shiller/data.htm.

Robert Shiller website: http://www.econ.yale.edu/~shiller/.

Jeremy Siegel, *The Future for Investors* (New York: Crown Business, 2005).

Jeremy Siegel, *Stocks for the Long Run*, 4th ed. (New York: McGraw-Hill, 2007).

Jeremy Siegel website: http://www.jeremysiegel.com/.

John Burr Williams, *The Theory of Investment Value* (Cambridge: Harvard University Press, 1938).

Jason Zweig, "The Intelligent Investor" column in the *Wall Street Journal*.

Index

Page numbers in italics refer to figures and tables.
Page numbers with n indicate note.